Trip Around the World **Wall Hanging**

MATERIALS:
Cotton fabric for pieces A through M, 66cm by 22cm each. Sheeting: navy for lining, 117cm by 133cm; lavender, 28cm by 110cm; purple, 28cm by 120cm. White sewing thread. Polyester batting.

DIRECTIONS:
1. Cut out patches, adding 0.7cm seam allowance all around. Following Piecing Diagram, sew patches together.
2. For border, sew strips to each side.
3. Place batting between pieced top and lining. Pin and baste three layers together. Quilt each patch, using white sewing thread.
4. Bind edges to finish.

Patterns Cut out adding 0.7cm seam allowance.

Sewing pieces together

A—K   48 pieces each

L   47 pieces

M   46 pieces

To begin and end off, make a simple backstitch. Sew patches in horizontal rows.

Sew long rows together, taking care to make corners meet. Press seams open.

Cutting Figures in parentheses indicate seam allowance. Cut out, adding 1cm seam allowance unless otherwise indicated.

5 | Border   1 | Cut 2   (2.5)
└─────── 108 ───────┘

5 | Border   2   (2.5)   (2.5) Cut 2   (2.5)
└─────── 102 ───────┘

5 | Edging   3 | Cut 2
└─────── 118 ───────┘

5 | Edging   4 | Cut 2
└─────── 107 ───────┘

Trim batting and lining edges to match.

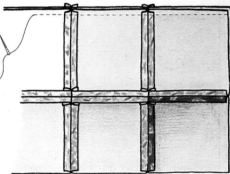

Slip-stitch
Wrong side

Sew in numerical order.

Piecing Diagram

Cut navy lining and batting to required size, adding 5cm all around to allow for final binging.

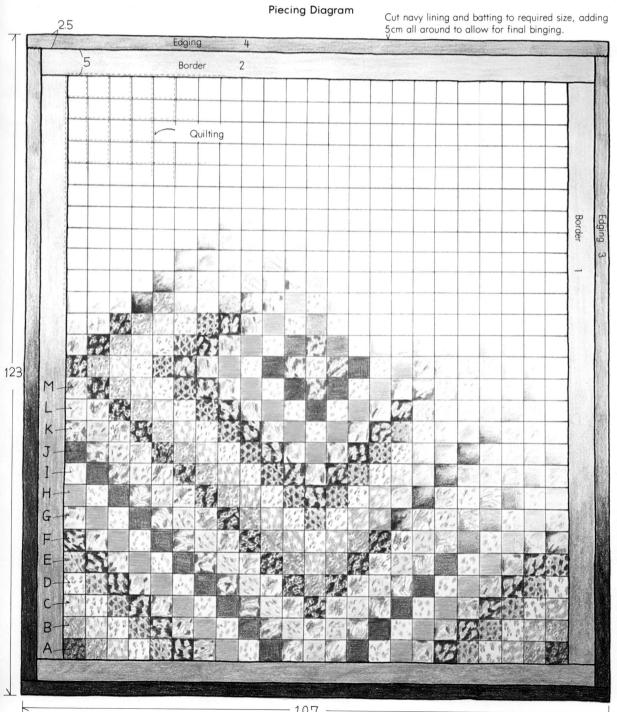

2.5

5

Edging   4

Border   2

Quilting

Border   1

Edging   3

123

M
L
K
J
I
H
G
F
E
D
C
B
A

107

3

Nine-Patch Pillows

Patterns

Cut out adding 1 cm seam allowance.

14

14

Sewing pieces together

A

Sew patches in numerical order.
Refer to pattern A for patterns B, C, and D.

① ② ① ② ①

③

① ② ① ② ①

③

① ② ① ② ①

To make pillow

Cut out adding 1 cm seam allowance.

Wrong side

Cut 2

Sheeting

42

21

Sew with right sides of front and back together.

Zipper

34 cm

Leave opening for zipper

With right sides of front and back together, stitch all around, taking ample allowance at corners as shwon.

1 cm

2 cm

Right side

Inner pillow

Cut 1

Fold

47

47

Cut piece for inner pillow a little larger than the size of outer pillow.

With right sides together, stitch all around leaving 15 cm open for turning.

Fold

15 cm

Opening for stuffing

Turn to right side. Stuff with kapok and slip-stitch opening.

MATERIALS:
For Pillow A: Sheeting: lavender, 60cm square; purple, 38cm by 76cm. Cotton print, 60cm by 32cm. For B: Beige sheeting, 62cm by 76cm. Cotton print, 60cm by 32cm. For C: Pink sheeting, 62cm by 60cm. Cotton prints: pink, 54cm by 32cm; pink and green, 38cm by 32cm. For D: Blue sheeting, 65cm square. Cotton prints: blue, 38cm by 16cm; dark blue, 16cm square. 400g of kapok and 34cm zipper for each pillow.

DIRECTICNS:
1. Add 0.7cm seam allowance all around. Cut patches and sew together following Piecing Diagram. Press seams open.
2. Cut out two pieces for back and sew in zipper. With right sides of front and back together, stitch all around. Turn to right side. Insert inner pillow.

Pillow A Piecing Diagram B

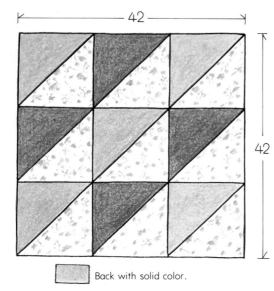

 42

42

Back with solid color.

Back with solid color.

C

D

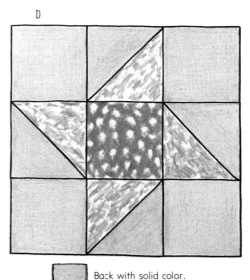

 Back with solid color.

Back with solid color.

Broken Dishes Crib Quilt and Tote Bag

MATERIALS:
For Crib Quilt: Fabric for patch E, 90cm by 250cm; for patches A and B, 90cm by 50cm each; for patches C and D, 90cm by 30cm each; for patch F, 90cm by 20cm. Polyester batting. Orange sewing thread. For Tote Bag: Canvas, 88cm by 125cm. Cotton fabric: yellow check, moss green check, moss green and yellow green, 30cm by 40cm each. Cotton print for lining, 88cm by 52cm. 40cm zipper. Four D-shape buckles, 2.5cm wide.

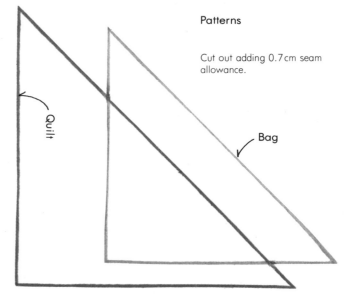

Patterns

Cut out adding 0.7cm seam allowance.

Quilt

Bag

Sewing pieces together   Sew in numerical order.

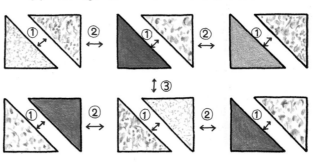

DIRECTIONS for Crib Quilt:
1. Following Piecing Diagram, sew patches together. Press seams open.
2. Place batting between quilt top and lining. Pin and baste through all thicknesses. To finish edges, fold excess fabric of lining to front of quilt top. Turn in raw edges and slip-stitch to quilt top, mitering corners.
3. Quilt each print triangle as shown, using white sewing thread.

Quilt   Piecing Diagram   Cut out patch pieces adding 0.7cm seam allowance to each piece.

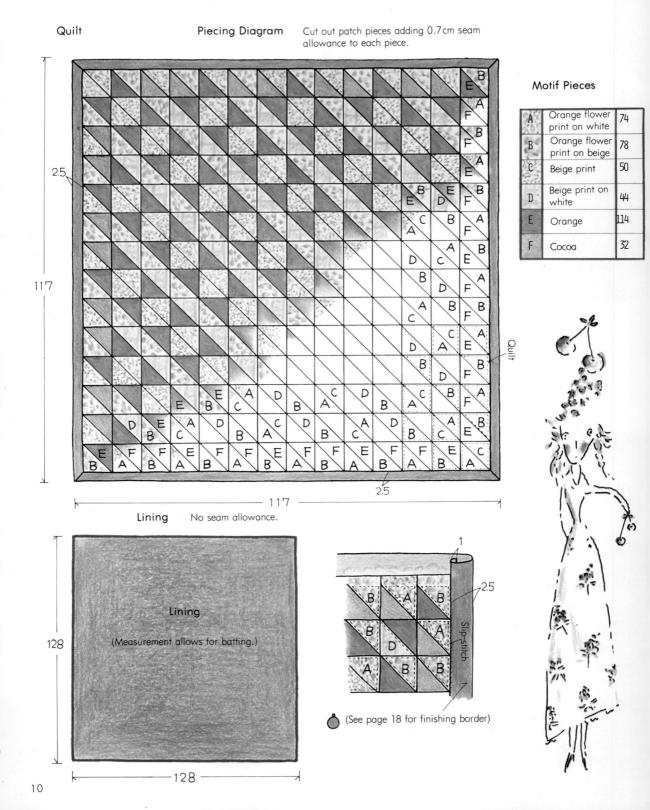

Motif Pieces

A	Orange flower print on white	74
B	Orange flower print on beige	78
C	Beige print	50
D	Beige print on white	44
E	Orange	114
F	Cocoa	32

2.5

117

2.5

117

Quilt

Lining   No seam allowance.

Lining

(Measurement allows for batting.)

128

128

1

2.5

Slip-stitch

(See page 18 for finishing border)

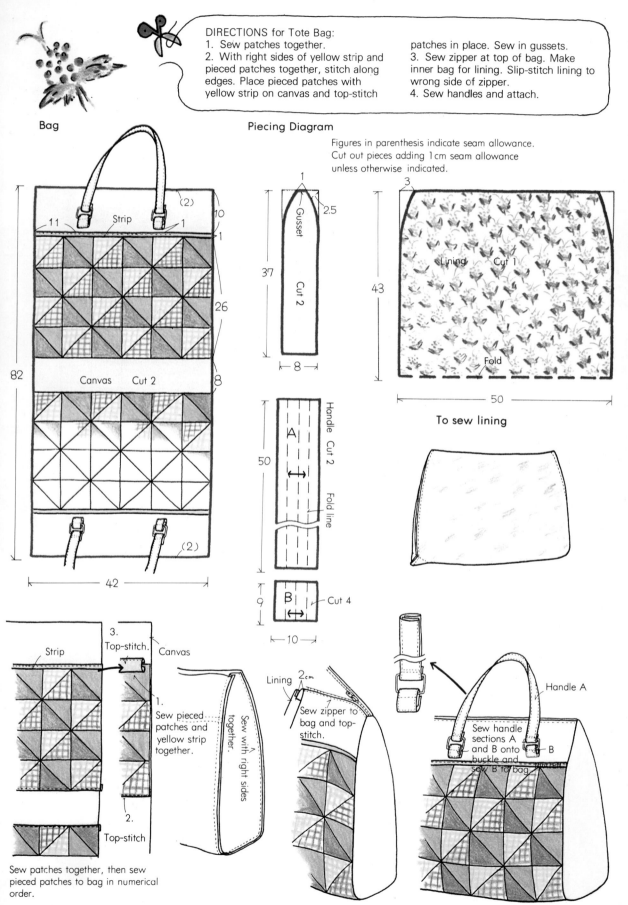

DIRECTIONS for Tote Bag:
1. Sew patches together.
2. With right sides of yellow strip and pieced patches together, stitch along edges. Place pieced patches with yellow strip on canvas and top-stitch patches in place. Sew in gussets.
3. Sew zipper at top of bag. Make inner bag for lining. Slip-stitch lining to wrong side of zipper.
4. Sew handles and attach.

Bag

Piecing Diagram

Figures in parenthesis indicate seam allowance.
Cut out pieces adding 1cm seam allowance
unless otherwise indicated.

(2)
11 Strip 1
10
1
26
Canvas Cut 2
8
82
(2)
42

1
2.5
Gusset
Cut 2
37
8

Handle Cut 2
A
50
Fold line

B Cut 4
9
10

3
Lining Cut 1
43
Fold
50

To sew lining

Strip
3. Top-stitch. Canvas
1. Sew pieced patches and yellow strip together.
Sew with right sides together.
2.
Top-stitch

Lining 2cm
Sew zipper to bag and top-stitch.

Handle A
Sew handle sections A and B onto buckle and sew B to bag.
B

Sew patches together, then sew pieced patches to bag in numerical order.

11

Old Maid's Puzzle Crib Quilt

and Shoulder Bag

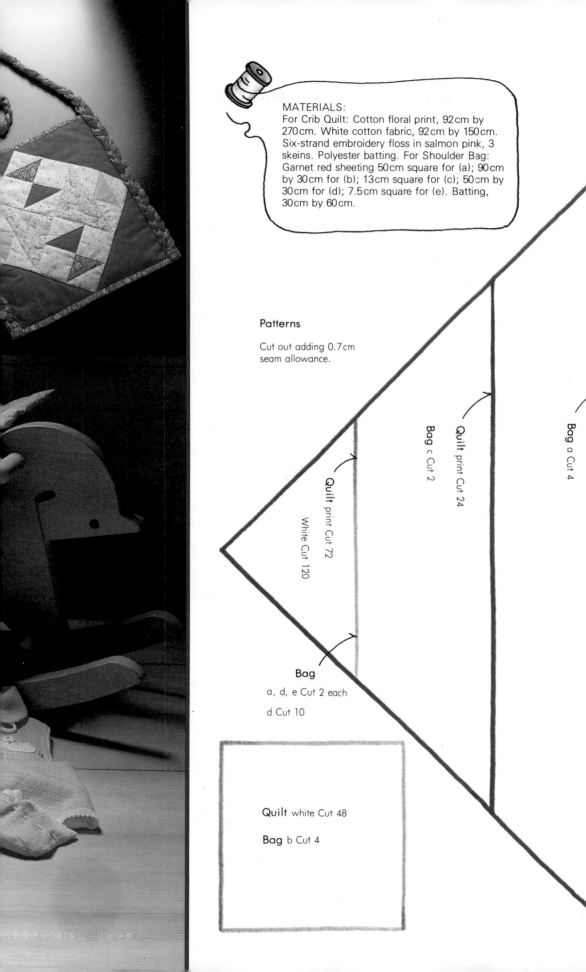

MATERIALS:
For Crib Quilt: Cotton floral print, 92cm by 270cm. White cotton fabric, 92cm by 150cm. Six-strand embroidery floss in salmon pink, 3 skeins. Polyester batting. For Shoulder Bag: Garnet red sheeting 50cm square for (a); 90cm by 30cm for (b); 13cm square for (c); 50cm by 30cm for (d); 7.5cm square for (e). Batting, 30cm by 60cm.

Patterns

Cut out adding 0.7cm seam allowance.

Bag a Cut 4

Quilt print Cut 24

Bag c Cut 2

Quilt print Cut 72

White Cut 120

Bag

a, d, e Cut 2 each

d Cut 10

Quilt white Cut 48

Bag b Cut 4

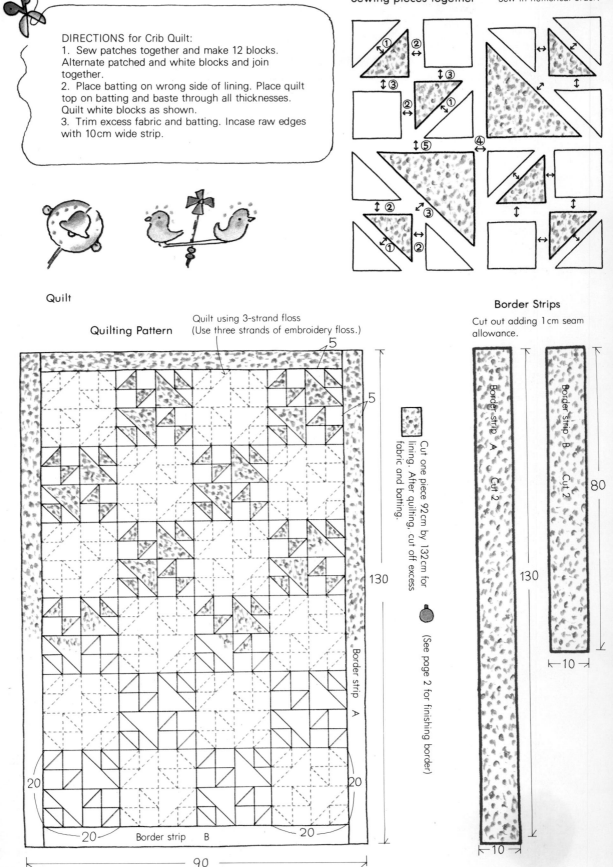

DIRECTIONS for Crib Quilt:
1. Sew patches together and make 12 blocks. Alternate patched and white blocks and join together.
2. Place batting on wrong side of lining. Place quilt top on batting and baste through all thicknesses. Quilt white blocks as shown.
3. Trim excess fabric and batting. Incase raw edges with 10cm wide strip.

Sewing pieces together   Sew in numerical order.

Quilt

Quilting Pattern

Quilt using 3-strand floss
(Use three strands of embroidery floss.)

Cut one piece 92cm by 132cm for lining. After quilting, cut off excess fabric and batting.

(See page 2 for finishing border)

Border strip   A

Border strip   B

5

5

130

20

20

20

20

90

Border Strips

Cut out adding 1cm seam allowance.

Border strip A   Cut 2

Border strip B   Cut 2

80

130

10

10

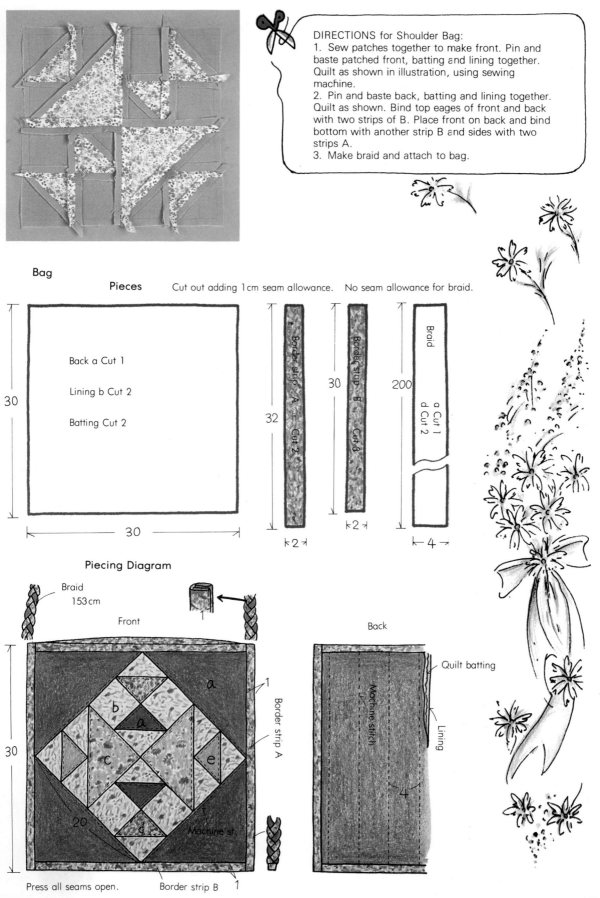

DIRECTIONS for Shoulder Bag:
1. Sew patches together to make front. Pin and baste patched front, batting and lining together. Quilt as shown in illustration, using sewing machine.
2. Pin and baste back, batting and lining together. Quilt as shown. Bind top edges of front and back with two strips of B. Place front on back and bind bottom with another strip B and sides with two strips A.
3. Make braid and attach to bag.

Bag

Pieces

Cut out adding 1cm seam allowance.   No seam allowance for braid.

Back a Cut 1

Lining b Cut 2

Batting Cut 2

30

30

Border strip A   Cut 2

32

2

Border strip B   Cut 3

30

2

Braid

a Cut 1
d Cut 2

200

4

Piecing Diagram

Braid
153cm

Front

a
b
a
c
e
d

1

Border strip A

Machine st.

30

20

Press all seams open.

Border strip B   1

Back

Quilt batting

Machine stitch

Lining

4

30

Drunkard's Path Table Center and Tote Bag

MATERIALS:
For Table Center: Cotton fabric: rose pink and floral print, 92cm by 130cm each; moss green for lining, 92cm by 216cm. White sewing thread. For Tote Bag: Cotton fabric: dark brown, 92cm by 40cm; floral print for (a) and (b), 80cm by 20cm each; print for lining, 80cm by 35cm. Batting, 60cm by 30cm. White sewing thread. Wooden handles.

Patterns   Cut out adding 0.7cm seam allowance.

Table Center

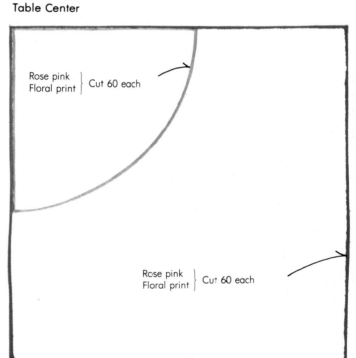

Rose pink
Floral print } Cut 60 each

Rose pink
Floral print } Cut 60 each

Bag

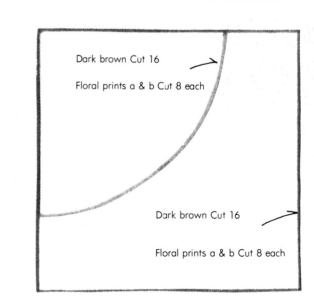

Dark brown Cut 16

Floral prints a & b Cut 8 each

Dark brown Cut 16

Floral prints a & b Cut 8 each

17

DIRECTIONS for Table Center:

1. Following illustration, sew small patch to large patch along curved edges. Make 120 squares, 60 of large flokal print and small rose pink, and 60 with colors reversed. Assemble squares as shown in Piecing Diagram, using tiny running stitches.

Press seams open.

2. Place pieced top on lining. Top-stitch with running stitch using white sewing thread as shown.

3. Fold excess fabric of lining to back and miter corners. Turn to right side and top- stitch by machine.

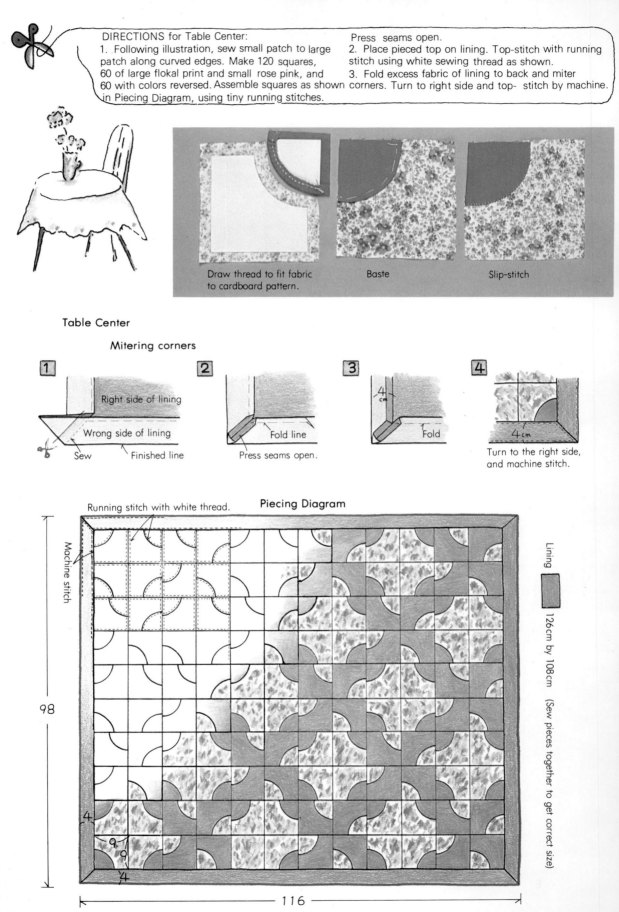

Draw thread to fit fabric to cardboard pattern.

Baste

Slip-stitch

Table Center

Mitering corners

1. Right side of lining — Wrong side of lining — Sew — Finished line

2. Fold line — Press seams open.

3. 4 cm — Fold

4. 4 cm — Turn to the right side, and machine stitch.

Piecing Diagram

Running stitch with white thread.

Machine stitch

Lining

126 cm by 108 cm (Sew pieces together to get correct size)

98

4

9

4

116

18

DIRECTIONS for Tote Bag:
1. Make 16 blocks. Following illustration, assemble blocks together. Place pieced blocks on batting. Quilt each square as shown. Make another piece for back in same manner.

2. Sew border pieces to quilted piece. With right sides of front and back together, stitch as indicated. Make inner bag. Insert inner bag into outer bag. Fold top edge over handle and slip-stitch lining to outer bag.

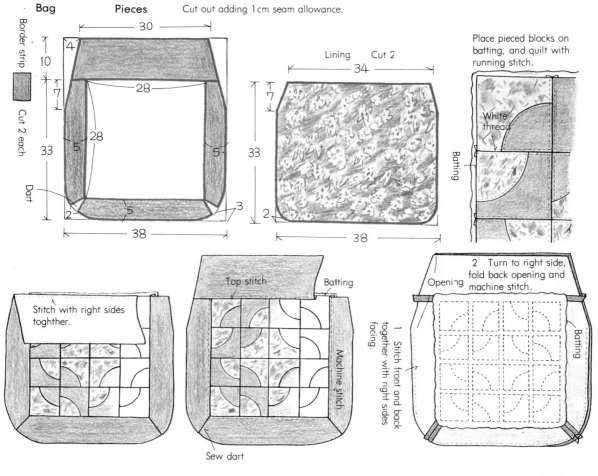

Bag **Pieces** Cut out adding 1 cm seam allowance.

Border strip
Cut 2 each

30 · 4 · 10 · 28 · 7 · 28 · 33 · 5 · 5 · Dart · 2 · 5 · 3 · 38

Lining Cut 2
34 · 7 · 33 · 2 · 38

Place pieced blocks on batting, and quilt with running stitch.
White thread
Batting

Stitch with right sides togther.

Top stitch · Batting · Machine stitch · Sew dart

2 Turn to right side, fold back opening and machine stitch.
Opening
1 Stitch front and back together with right sides facing.
Batting

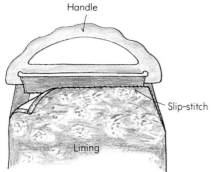

Handle
Slip-stitch
Lining

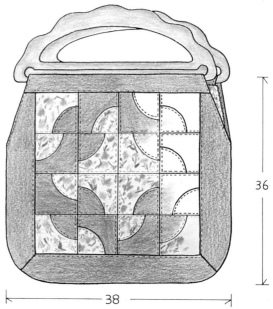

36

38

Tumbling Blocks Tablecloth and Pillow

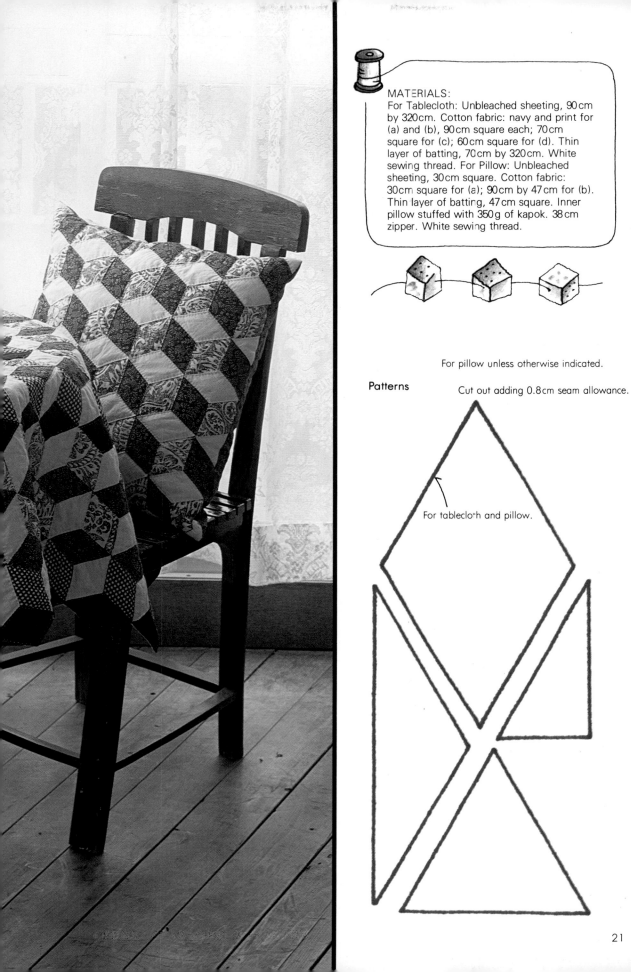

MATERIALS:
For Tablecloth: Unbleached sheeting, 90 cm by 320 cm. Cotton fabric: navy and print for (a) and (b), 90 cm square each; 70 cm square for (c); 60 cm square for (d). Thin layer of batting, 70 cm by 320 cm. White sewing thread. For Pillow: Unbleached sheeting, 30 cm square. Cotton fabric: 30 cm square for (a); 90 cm by 47 cm for (b). Thin layer of batting, 47 cm square. Inner pillow stuffed with 350 g of kapok. 38 cm zipper. White sewing thread.

For pillow unless otherwise indicated.

Patterns

Cut out adding 0.8 cm seam allowance.

For tablecloth and pillow.

Tablecloth

Block A Cut 121

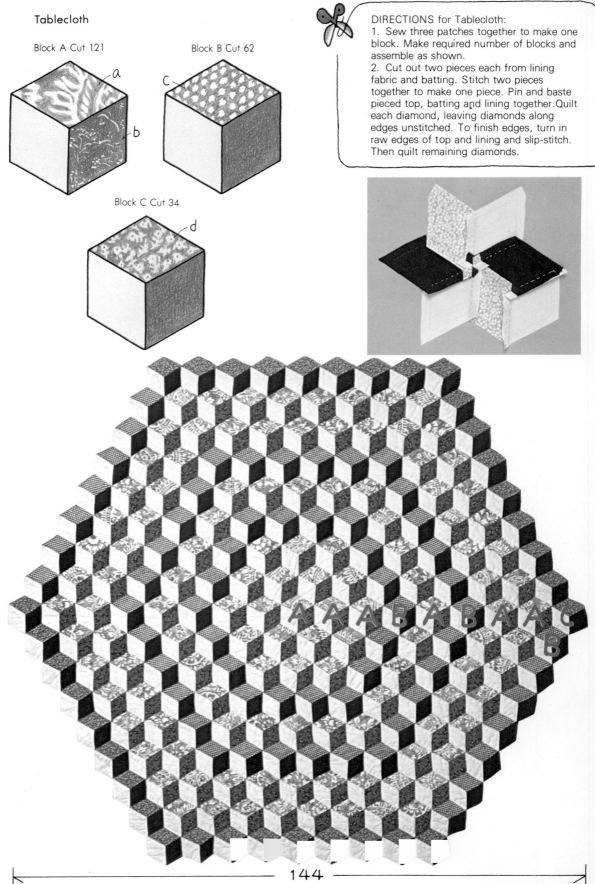

a

b

Block B Cut 62

C

Block C Cut 34

d

DIRECTIONS for Tablecloth:
1. Sew three patches together to make one block. Make required number of blocks and assemble as shown.
2. Cut out two pieces each from lining fabric and batting. Stitch two pieces together to make one piece. Pin and baste pieced top, batting and lining together. Quilt each diamond, leaving diamonds along edges unstitched. To finish edges, turn in raw edges of top and lining and slip-stitch. Then quilt remaining diamonds.

144

Lining

No seam allowance.

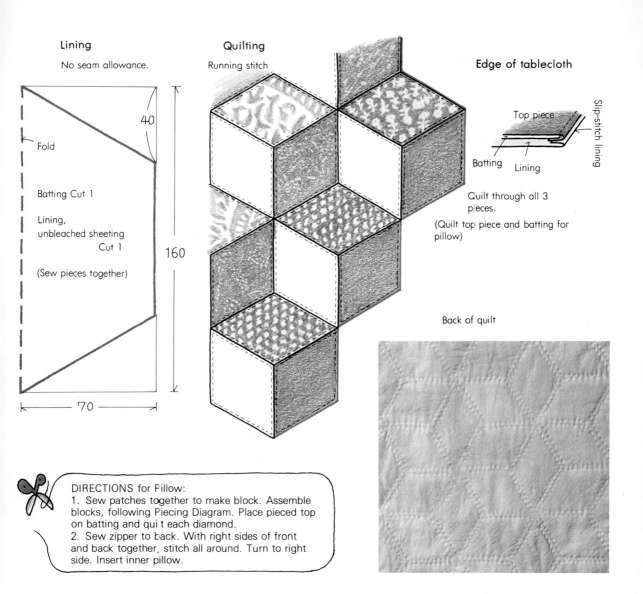

40

Fold

Batting Cut 1

Lining,
unbleached sheeting
Cut 1

(Sew pieces together)

160

70

Quilting

Running stitch

Edge of tablecloth

Top piece

Slip-stitch lining

Batting   Lining

Quilt through all 3 pieces.

(Quilt top piece and batting for pillow)

Back of quilt

DIRECTIONS for Fillow:
1. Sew patches together to make block. Assemble blocks, following Piecing Diagram. Place pieced top on batting and quit each diamond.
2. Sew zipper to back. With right sides of front and back together, stitch all around. Turn to right side. Insert inner pillow.

Pillow

Piecing Diagram

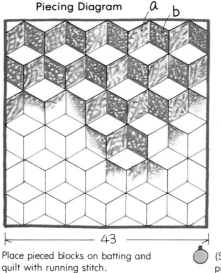

a b

45

43

Place pieced blocks on batting and quilt with running stitch.

(See page 6 for inner pillow)

Back b

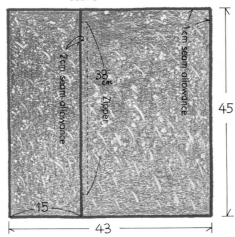

2cm seam allowance

30cm
Zipper

1cm seam allowance

45

15

43

Sew in zipper, and with right sidesof front and back together, stitch all around edges.

Odd Fellows Patch

Tablecloth and Pillow

MATERIALS:
For Tablecloth: Cotton fabric: blue, 60cm by 112cm; pale blue print, 90cm by 130cm; light gray, 90cm by 70cm; dark gray, 90cm by 60cm. Unbleached sheeting for lining, 110cm square. For Pillow: Sheeting: dark brown, 90cm by 50cm; golden brown, 40cm by 20cm. Cotton print, 50cm by 35cm. 38cm zipper. Inner pillow stuffed with 450g of kapok.

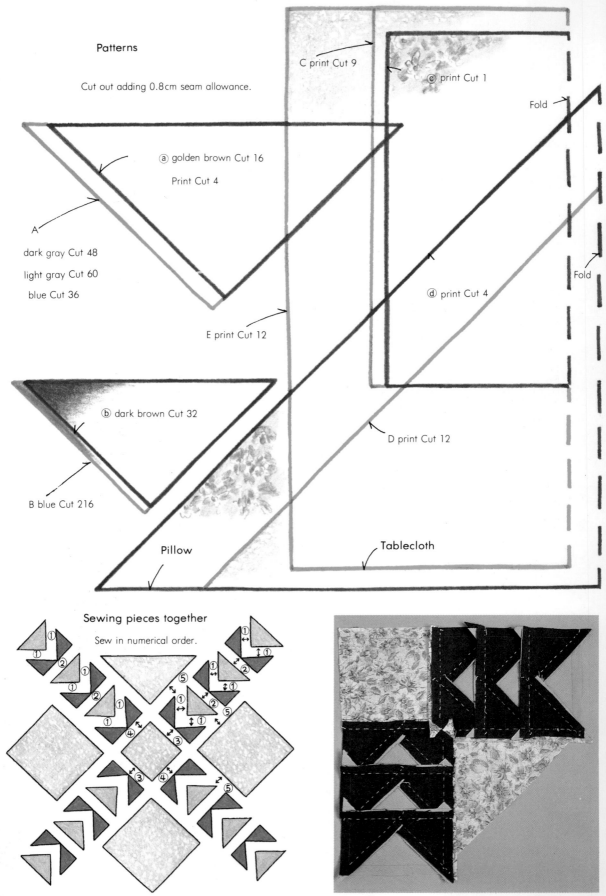

Patterns

Cut out adding 0.8cm seam allowance.

C print Cut 9

ⓒ print Cut 1

Fold

ⓐ golden brown Cut 16

Print Cut 4

A

dark gray Cut 48

light gray Cut 60

blue Cut 36

Fold

ⓓ print Cut 4

E print Cut 12

ⓑ dark brown Cut 32

D print Cut 12

B blue Cut 216

Pillow

Tablecloth

Sewing pieces together

Sew in numerical order.

26

DIRECTIONS for Tablecloth:
1. Sew patches together, following Piecing Diagram. Press seams to one side.
2. Place patched top on lining, with wrong sides together, and incase raw edges with 5cm wide strip.

DIRECTIONS for Pillow:
1. Sew patches together. Sew border strip to patched piece all around, mitering corners.
2. Sew zipper to back. With right sides of front and back together, stitch all around. Turn to right side. Insert inner pillow.

Tablecloth

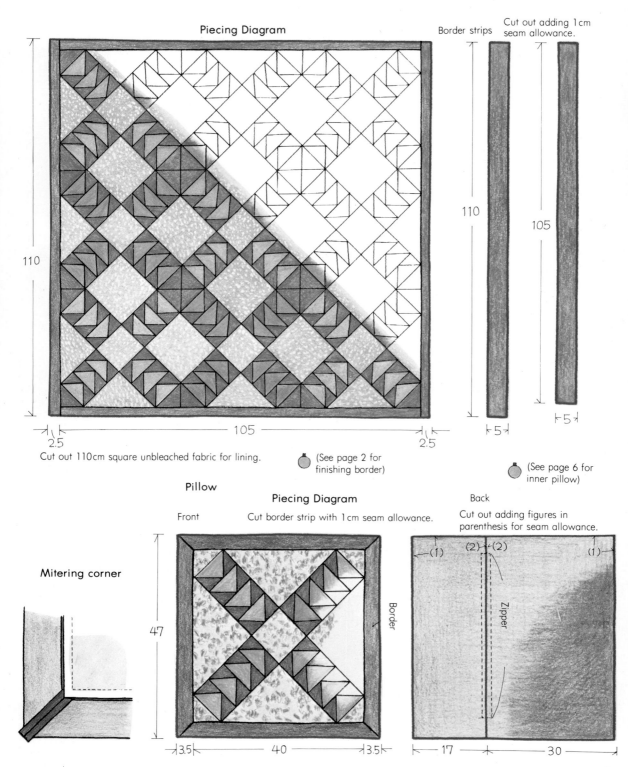

Piecing Diagram

110

105

2.5   2.5

Cut out 110cm square unbleached fabric for lining.

(See page 2 for finishing border)

Border strips   Cut out adding 1cm seam allowance.

110   105

5   5

(See page 6 for inner pillow)

Pillow

Piecing Diagram

Front   Cut border strip with 1cm seam allowance.

Back
Cut out adding figures in parenthesis for seam allowance.

Mitering corner

47

3.5   40   3.5

Border

(1) (2) (2)   (1)

Zipper

17   30

Rose Garden Pillows and Tote Bags

MATERIALS:
For One Pillow: Olive green sheeting for (g), 60cm by 64cm. Cotton fabric: 22cm square for (e); 16cm square for (d); 12cm square for (c); 10cm square for (b); 7cm square for (a); 28cm square for (f). 32cm zipper. Inner pillow stuffed with 250g of kapok. For Tote Bag: Quilted cotton floral print in pink (dark brown), 80cm square. Sheeting: olive green (dark brown), 40cm by 10cm; 30cm by 18cm each for C and E; 29cm by 16cm each for B and D; 8cm square for A. Bias binding tape in pink (dark brown), 180cm long. Six-strand embroidery floss in pink (golden yellow).

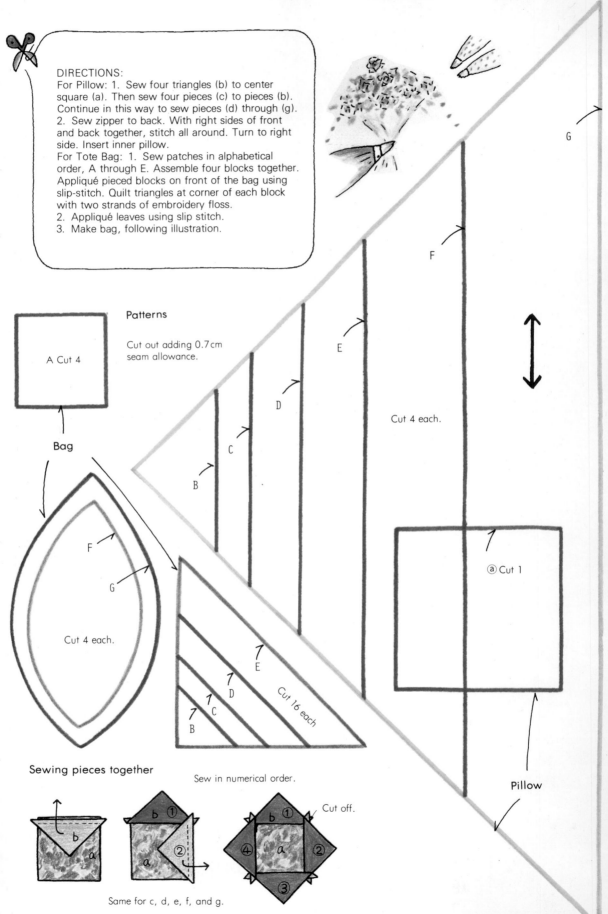

DIRECTIONS:

For Pillow: 1. Sew four triangles (b) to center square (a). Then sew four pieces (c) to pieces (b). Continue in this way to sew pieces (d) through (g).
2. Sew zipper to back. With right sides of front and back together, stitch all around. Turn to right side. Insert inner pillow.

For Tote Bag: 1. Sew patches in alphabetical order, A through E. Assemble four blocks together. Appliqué pieced blocks on front of the bag using slip-stitch. Quilt triangles at corner of each block with two strands of embroidery floss.
2. Appliqué leaves using slip stitch.
3. Make bag, following illustration.

Patterns

Cut out adding 0.7 cm seam allowance.

A Cut 4

Bag

G

F

E

D

C

B

F

G

Cut 4 each.

E

D

C

B

Cut 16 each

Cut 4 each.

ⓐ Cut 1

Pillow

Sewing pieces together

Sew in numerical order.

Cut off.

Same for c, d, e, f, and g.

Pillow

Piecing Diagram

Figures in parentheses indicate seam allowance.
Cut out adding 1 cm seam allowance unless otherwise indicated.

 See page 6 for inner pillow.

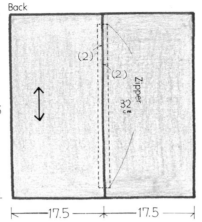

Front

35

35

Back

(2)

(2)

Zipper 32 cm

17.5 — 17.5

Bag

Piecing Diagram

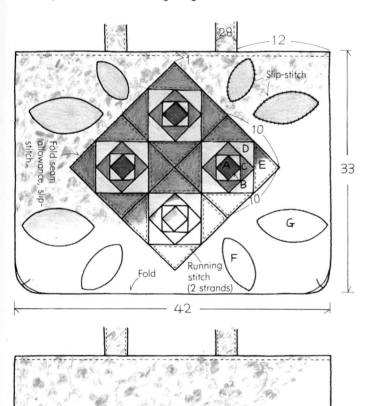

28

12

Slip-stitch

10

D
A C E
B

10

Fold seam allowance, slip-stitch

G

F

Fold

Running stitch (2 strands)

33

42

Bag pieces

Cotton floral print.

Figures in parentheses indicate seam allowance.
Cut out adding 1 cm seam allowance unless otherwise indicated.

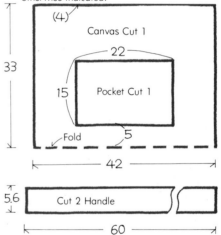

(4)

Canvas Cut 1

22

33

15

Pocket Cut 1

Fold

5

42

5.6

Cut 2 Handle

60

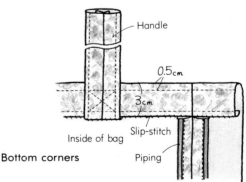

Handle

0.5 cm

3 cm

Inside of bag

Slip-stitch

Piping

Bias binding tape

Inside of pocket

Bottom corners

Stitch

4

31

Mosaic
Table Center
and Telephone Set

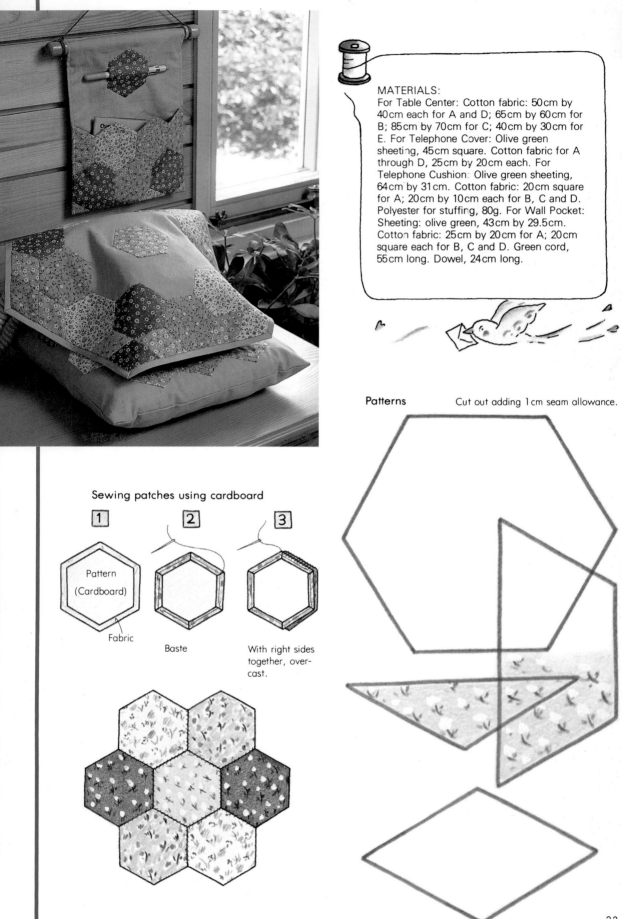

Patterns   Cut out adding 1cm seam allowance.

Sewing patches using cardboard

1 2 3

Pattern
(Cardboard)

Fabric

Baste

With right sides
together, over-
cast.

33

DIRECTIONS:

For Table Center: 1. Place cardboard pattern on wrong side of patch. Turn seam allowance over cardboard and baste. With right sides of backed patches together, overcast along edges. Remove cardboard after pieces are joined.

2. Overcast edges of hexagons for back and front together. Turn to back. Slip-stitch edges of hexagons to lining. For Telephone Set: Make Cover, Wall Pocket and Cushion, following illustration.

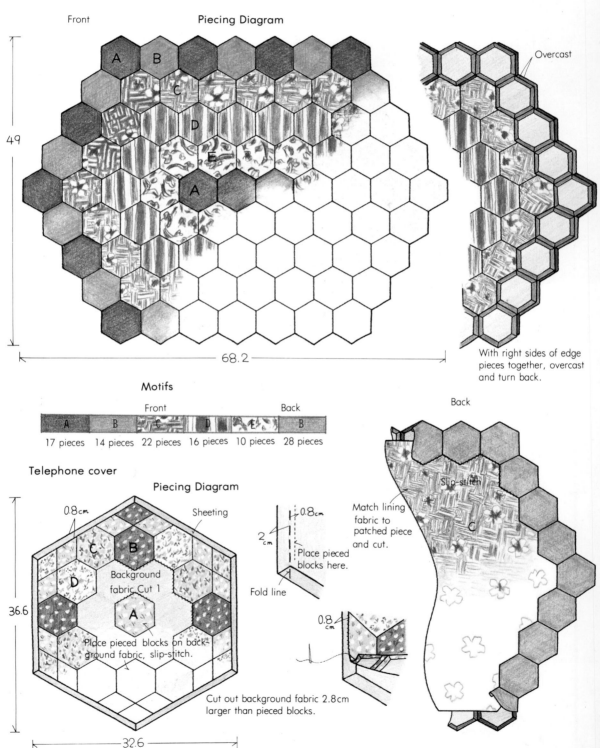

Table Center

Front

Piecing Diagram

49

68.2

Overcast

With right sides of edge pieces together, overcast and turn back.

Motifs

Front					Back
A	B	C	D	E	B
17 pieces	14 pieces	22 pieces	16 pieces	10 pieces	28 pieces

Back

Slip-stitch

Match lining fabric to patched piece and cut.

C

Telephone cover

Piecing Diagram

0.8cm

Sheeting

C

B

Background fabric Cut 1

D

A

36.6

Place pieced blocks on background fabric, slip-stitch.

0.8cm

2cm

Place pieced blocks here.

Fold line

0.8cm

Cut out background fabric 2.8cm larger than pieced blocks.

32.6

Telephone cushion   Piecing Diagram   Cut out adding 1cm seam allowance.

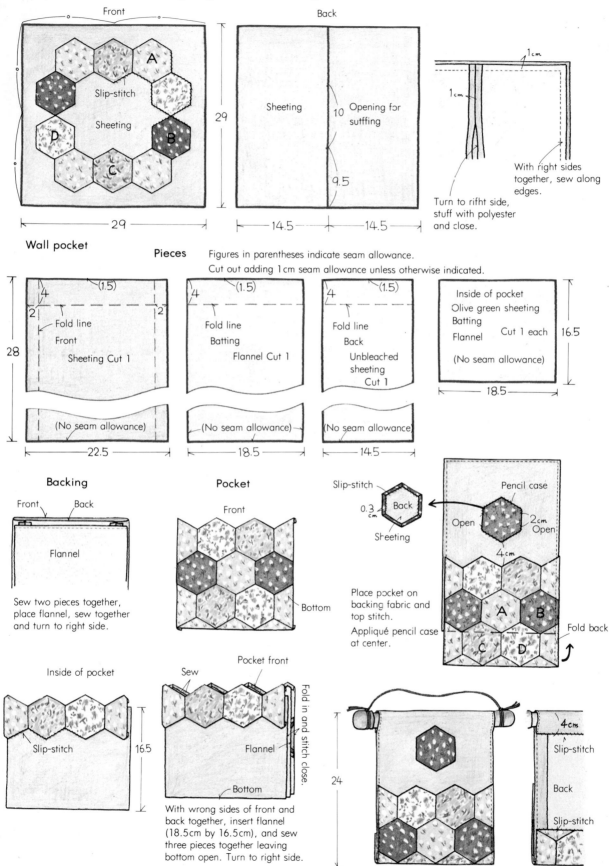

Front

A

Slip-stitch

Sheeting

D

B

C

29

29

Back

Sheeting

10 Opening for sutffing

9.5

14.5   14.5

1cm

1cm

With right sides together, sew along edges.

Turn to rifht side, stuff with polyester and close.

Wall pocket

Pieces   Figures in parentheses indicate seam allowance.
Cut out adding 1cm seam allowance unless otherwise indicated.

(1.5)

4

2   2

Fold line

Front

Sheeting Cut 1

28

(No seam allowance)

22.5

(1.5)

4

Fold line

Batting

Flannel Cut 1

(No seam allowance)

18.5

(1.5)

4

Fold line

Back

Unbleached sheeting Cut 1

(No seam allowance)

14.5

Inside of pocket
Olive green sheeting
Batting
Flannel   Cut 1 each

(No seam allowance)

16.5

18.5

Backing

Front   Back

Flannel

Sew two pieces together, place flannel, sew together and turn to right side.

Pocket

Front

Bottom

Slip-stitch

0.3 cm   Back

Open

Sheeting

Pencil case

2cm Open

4cm

A   B

C   D

Place pocket on backing fabric and top stitch.

Appliqué pencil case at center.

Fold back

Inside of pocket

Slip-stitch

16.5

Sew

Pocket front

Flannel

Bottom

Fold in and stitch close.

With wrong sides of front and back together, insert flannel (18.5cm by 16.5cm), and sew three pieces together leaving bottom open. Turn to right side.

24

4cm

Slip-stitch

Back

Slip-stitch

North Carolina Lily Framed Patchwork and Shoulder Bag

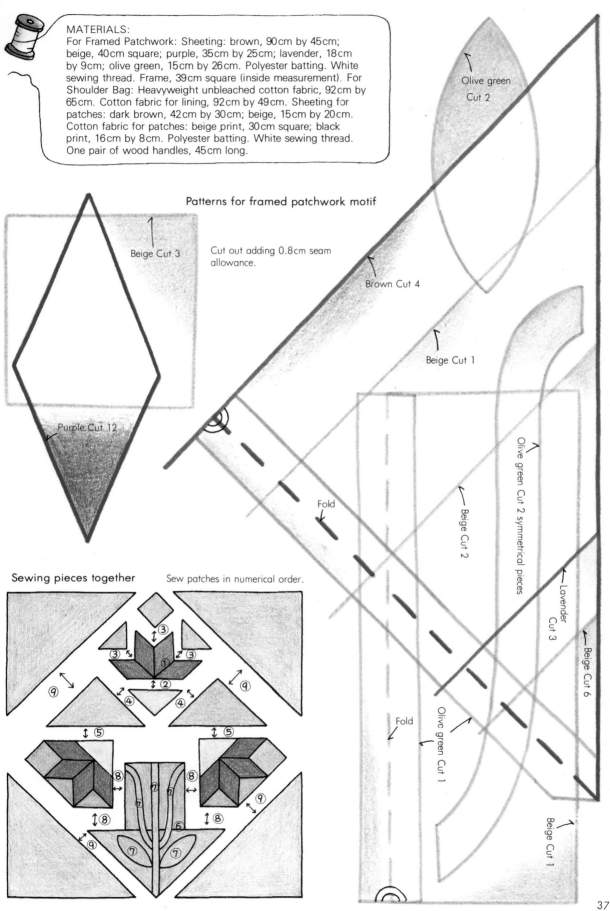

MATERIALS:
For Framed Patchwork: Sheeting: brown, 90cm by 45cm; beige, 40cm square; purple, 35cm by 25cm; lavender, 18cm by 9cm; olive green, 15cm by 26cm. Polyester batting. White sewing thread. Frame, 39cm square (inside measurement). For Shoulder Bag: Heavyweight unbleached cotton fabric, 92cm by 65cm. Cotton fabric for lining, 92cm by 49cm. Sheeting for patches: dark brown, 42cm by 30cm; beige, 15cm by 20cm. Cotton fabric for patches: beige print, 30cm square; black print, 16cm by 8cm. Polyester batting. White sewing thread. One pair of wood handles, 45cm long.

Patterns for framed patchwork motif

Beige Cut 3

Cut out adding 0.8cm seam allowance.

Purple Cut 12

Olive green Cut 2

Brown Cut 4

Beige Cut 1

Olive green Cut 2 symmetrical pieces

Beige Cut 2

Lavender Cut 3

Beige Cut 6

Fold

Fold

Olive green Cut 1

Beige Cut 1

Sewing pieces together   Sew patches in numerical order.

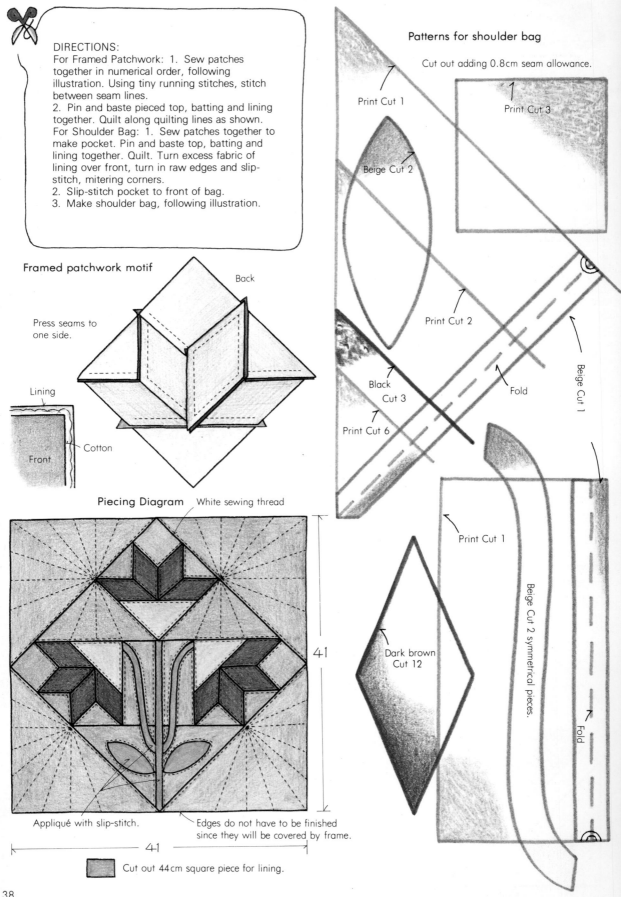

DIRECTIONS:
For Framed Patchwork: 1. Sew patches together in numerical order, following illustration. Using tiny running stitches, stitch between seam lines.
2. Pin and baste pieced top, batting and lining together. Quilt along quilting lines as shown.
For Shoulder Bag: 1. Sew patches together to make pocket. Pin and baste top, batting and lining together. Quilt. Turn excess fabric of lining over front, turn in raw edges and slip-stitch, mitering corners.
2. Slip-stitch pocket to front of bag.
3. Make shoulder bag, following illustration.

Framed patchwork motif

Back

Press seams to one side.

Lining

Cotton

Front

Piecing Diagram — White sewing thread

41

41

Appliqué with slip-stitch.

Edges do not have to be finished since they will be covered by frame.

Cut out 44cm square piece for lining.

Patterns for shoulder bag

Cut out adding 0.8cm seam allowance.

Print Cut 1

Print Cut 3

Beige Cut 2

Print Cut 2

Beige Cut 1

Black Cut 3

Fold

Print Cut 6

Print Cut 1

Dark brown Cut 12

Beige Cut 2 symmetrical pieces.

Fold

Shoulder bag

Pieces

Fold allowance 6cm

Front and Back
Top piece and lining
Cut 2 each

39

Seam allowance 1cm

47

Handle

Top Cut 2   Fold allowance
1cm

6

92

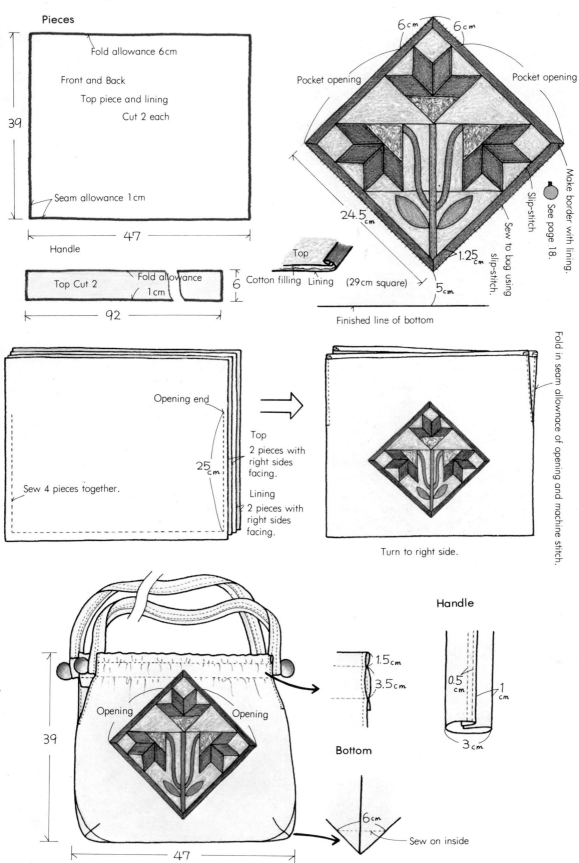

6cm   6cm

Pocket opening   Pocket opening

24.5cm

Make border with lining.

See page 18.

Slip-stitch

Sew to bag using slip-stitch.

1.25cm

5cm

Top   Cotton filling   Lining   (29cm square)

Finished line of bottom

Opening end

Sew 4 pieces together.

25cm

Top
2 pieces with right sides facing.

Lining
2 pieces with right sides facing.

Fold in seam allownace of opening and machine stitch.

Turn to right side.

Opening   Opening

39

47

1.5cm

3.5cm

Handle

0.5cm   1cm

3cm

Bottom

6cm   Sew on inside

Double Wedding Ring Quilt and Pillows

MATERIALS:

For Quilt: Cotton fabric: beige for top and print for lining, 90 cm by 460 cm each. Cotton fabric for patches: red, dark and light pink, orange for (d), 48 pieces each; prints for (a), (b) and (c), 384 pieces each; red for piping, 90 cm by 50 cm. Polyester batting. White sewing thread. For One Pillow: Cotton fabric: beige, 78 cm by 37 cm; small amounts of prints in different colors for patches; red for piping, 30 cm square. 30 cm zipper. Inner pillow stuffed with 200g of kapok. Six-strand embroidery floss in beige.

DIRECTIONS:

For Quilt: 1. Sew (a), (b), (c) and (d) together with overcast or whipping running stitch, following Piecing Diagram. Make 48 blocks each for A and B.
2. Appliqué blocks A and B on beige fabric using slip stitch, following Appliqué Diagram.
3. Pin and baste appliquéd top, batting and lining together. Quilt along quilting lines.
4. Trim excess fabric and batting, leaving 2.5cm from the finished line. Incase raw edges with bias binding tape all around.
For Pillow: 1. Make four blocks in same manner as for Quilt top. Embroider along quilting lines in running stitch, using three strands of embroidery floss in center.
2. Sew zipper to back. With wrong sides of front and back together, incase raw edges with bias binding tape. Insert inner pillow.

Patterns

Figures in parentheses are for pillow.
Cut out adding 0.7 cm seam allowance.

Quilting Pattern

D

Red, Orange,
Dark and pale pink

Cut 48 pieces each.

(Red and dark pink   Cut 4 pieces each)

C

384 pieces

(16 pieces)

B

384 pieces

(16 pieces)

A

384 pieces

(16 pieces)

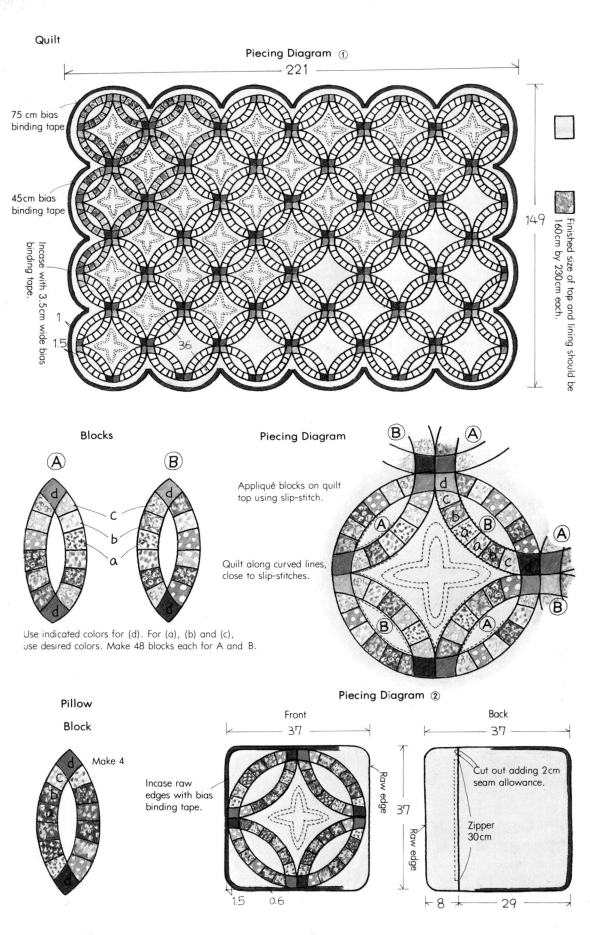

Quilt

Piecing Diagram ①

← 221 →

75 cm bias binding tape

45cm bias binding tape

Incase with 3.5cm wide bias binding tape.

1
1.5
36

149

Finished size of top and lining should be 160cm by 230cm each.

Blocks

Ⓐ

Ⓑ

d
c
b
a
d

Use indicated colors for (d). For (a), (b) and (c), use desired colors. Make 48 blocks each for A and B.

Piecing Diagram

Appliqué blocks on quilt top using slip-stitch.

Quilt along curved lines, close to slip-stitches.

Ⓑ Ⓐ
d
c
Ⓐ b Ⓑ
b
c
d Ⓐ
Ⓑ Ⓐ
Ⓑ

Pillow

Block

d
c
b
a
d

Make 4

Piecing Diagram ②

Front
← 37 →

Incase raw edges with bias binding tape.

1.5   0.6

Raw edge

Back
← 37 →

Cut out adding 2cm seam allowance.

37

Raw edge

Zipper 30cm

← 8 → ← 29 →

43

Dresden Plate Quilt

and Shoulder Bag

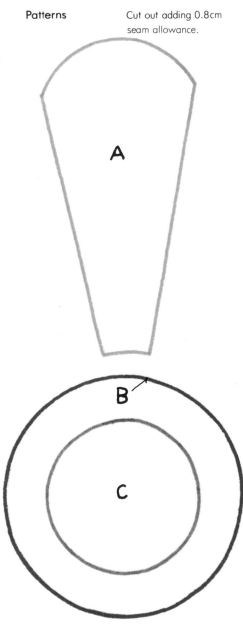

MATERIALS:
For Quilt: Sheeting: pink, 90cm by 360cm; dark pink, 90cm by 8cm; grayish purple, 20cm square. Cotton fabric: gray print, 90cm by 350cm; white print, 90cm by 40cm. Fabric for lining and thin layer of batting, 90cm by 460cm each. Six-strand embroidery floss in dark pink. For Shoulder Bag: Sheeting: blue, 41cm by 58cm; scrap of pink. Cotton print, 41cm by 70cm. Scrap of gingham check. Six-strand embroidery floss in blue.

Patterns Cut out adding 0.8cm seam allowance.

A

B

C

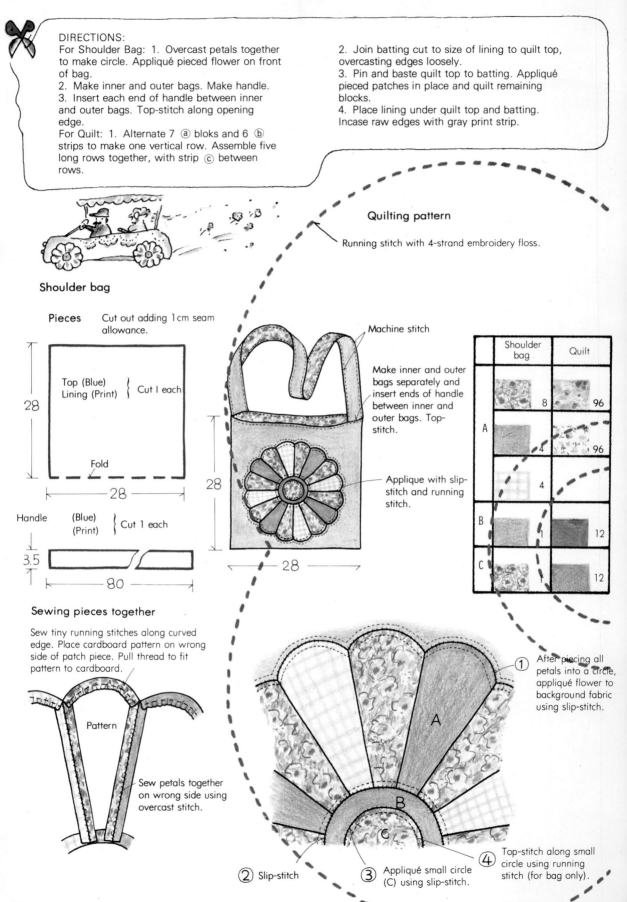

DIRECTIONS:

For Shoulder Bag: 1. Overcast petals together to make circle. Appliqué pieced flower on front of bag.
2. Make inner and outer bags. Make handle.
3. Insert each end of handle between inner and outer bags. Top-stitch along opening edge.

For Quilt: 1. Alternate 7 ⓐ bloks and 6 ⓑ strips to make one vertical row. Assemble five long rows together, with strip ⓒ between rows.

2. Join batting cut to size of lining to quilt top, overcasting edges loosely.
3. Pin and baste quilt top to batting. Appliqué pieced patches in place and quilt remaining blocks.
4. Place lining under quilt top and batting. Incase raw edges with gray print strip.

Shoulder bag

Pieces   Cut out adding 1cm seam allowance.

Top (Blue)
Lining (Print) } Cut 1 each

28

28

Fold

Handle   (Blue)
(Print) } Cut 1 each

3.5

80

Sewing pieces together

Sew tiny running stitches along curved edge. Place cardboard pattern on wrong side of patch piece. Pull thread to fit pattern to cardboard.

Pattern

Sew petals together on wrong side using overcast stitch.

Quilting pattern

Running stitch with 4-strand embroidery floss.

Machine stitch

Make inner and outer bags separately and insert ends of handle between inner and outer bags. Top-stitch.

Applique with slip-stitch and running stitch.

28

28

	Shoulder bag		Quilt	
A		8		96
A		4		96
A		4		
B		1		12
C				12

① After piecing all petals into a circle, appliqué flower to background fabric using slip-stitch.

A

B

C

② Slip-stitch

③ Appliqué small circle (C) using slip-stitch.

④ Top-stitch along small circle using running stitch (for bag only).

Quilt

Sequence for piecing top

③ Pin and baste quilt top to batting.

Piecing Diagram

Cut out adding 1.5cm seam allowance.

Lining

Batting
} 165cm by 229cm each.

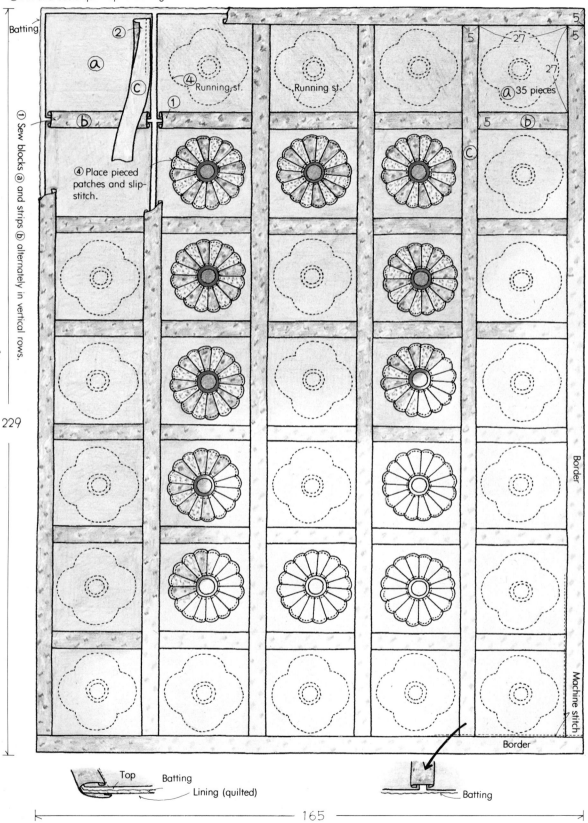

Batting

① Sew blocks ⓐ and strips ⓑ alternately in vertical rows.

229

②

ⓐ

ⓒ

ⓑ

④ Running st.

①

④ Place pieced patches and slip-stitch.

Running st.

Running st.

5

27

27

ⓐ 35 pieces

5

5

5

ⓑ

ⓒ

Border

Border

Machine stitch

Top

Batting

Lining (quilted)

Batting

165

Cathedral
Window
Pillow and
Tote Bag

To make Cathedral Window

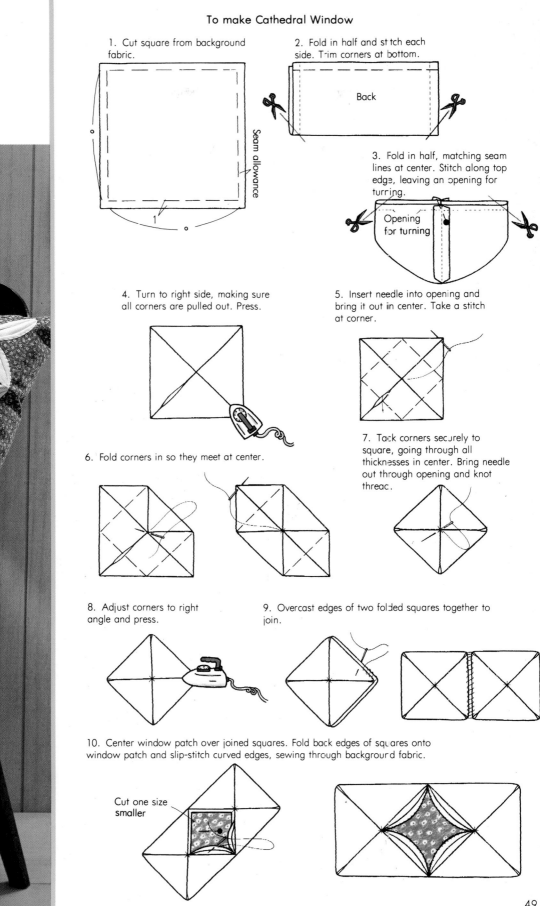

1. Cut square from background fabric.

2. Fold in half and stitch each side. Trim corners at bottom.

Back

Seam allowance

1

3. Fold in half, matching seam lines at center. Stitch along top edge, leaving an opening for turning.

Opening for turning

4. Turn to right side, making sure all corners are pulled out. Press.

5. Insert needle into opening and bring it out in center. Take a stitch at corner.

6. Fold corners in so they meet at center.

7. Tack corners securely to square, going through all thicknesses in center. Bring needle out through opening and knot thread.

8. Adjust corners to right angle and press.

9. Overcast edges of two folded squares together to join.

10. Center window patch over joined squares. Fold back edges of squares onto window patch and slip-stitch curved edges, sewing through background fabric.

Cut one size smaller

49

MATERIALS:
For Pillow: Cotton floral print with blue background, 90cm by 60cm. Unbleached sheeting, 90cm by 120cm. 36cm zipper. Inner pillow stuffed with 390g of kapok. For Tote Bag: Denim in navy, 92cm by 100cm. Cotton fabric: red print, 90cm by 70cm; blue for lining, 75cm by 70cm.

Pillow

Pieces

Figures in parentheses indicate seam allowance.
Cut out adding 1cm seam allowance unless otherwise indicated.
Do not add seam allowance for window patches unless otherwise indicated.

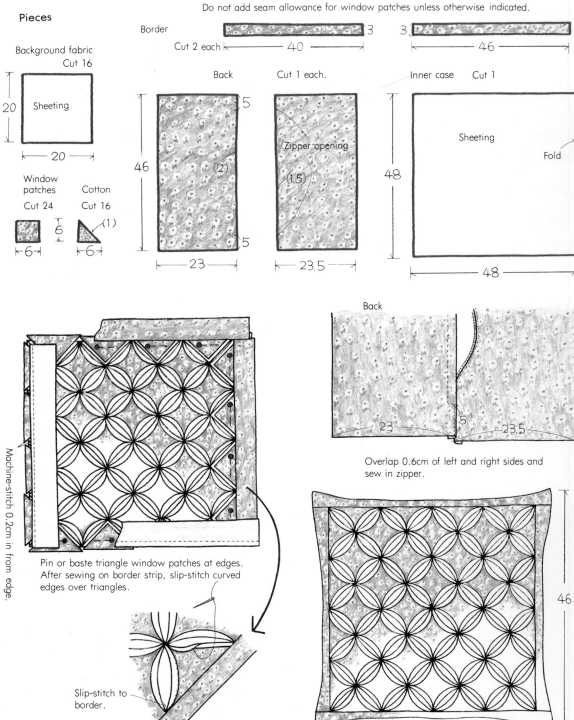

Background fabric
Cut 16

Sheeting
20
20

Window patches
Cut 24

Cotton
Cut 16

6
6
(1)
6

Border
Cut 2 each
40
3
3
46

Back
Cut 1 each.
5
46
(2)
23
Zipper opening
(1.5)
5
23.5

Inner case   Cut 1
Sheeting
48
Fold
48

Machine-stitch 0.2cm in from edge.

Pin or baste triangle window patches at edges. After sewing on border strip, slip-stitch curved edges over triangles.

Slip-stitch to border.

Back
23
5
23.5

Overlap 0.6cm of left and right sides and sew in zipper.

46
46

50

DIRECTIONS:

For Pillow: 1. Following directions for Cathedral Window, assemble four rows of four squares together. Place window patches on each square and corner triangle as shown. Sew strips for border close to edges.
2. Sew zipper to back.
3. With right sides of front and back together, stitch along edges.
For Bag: 1. Make center of bag in same manner as for Pillow. Assemble two rows of three squares together. Sew side pieces to center to make front. Make back piece in same manner as front.
2. Pin and baste triangle window patches at top and bottom. Sew gusset between front and back.
3. Make inner bag in same manner as outer bag. Insert inner bag into outer bag and slip-stitch inner bag to outer bag along each side.
4. Slip-stitch curved edges to triangle at top. Incase raw edges of inner and outer bags with 8cm wide strips.
5. Sew handles in place.

Bag

Pieces

Add 1cm seam allowance unless otherwise indicated.
Figures in parentheses indicate seam allowance.
Don't add seam allowance for window patches unless otherwise indicated.

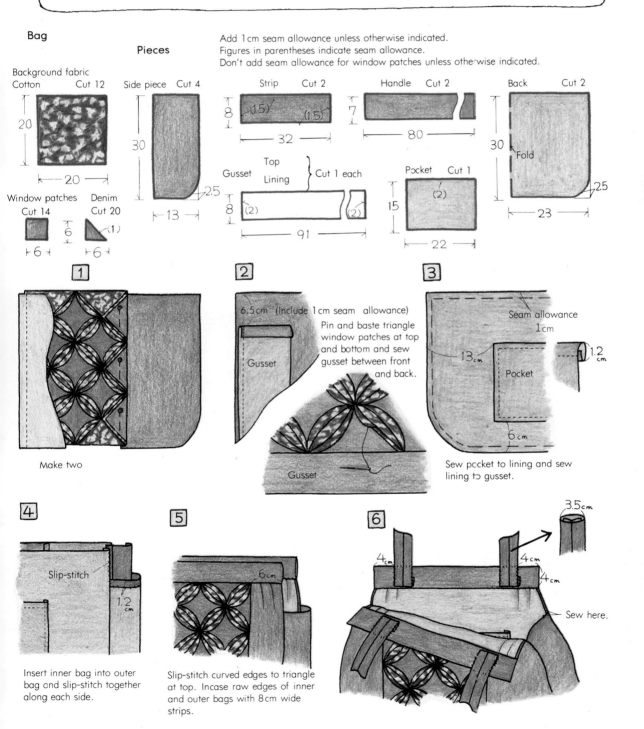

Background fabric
Cotton   Cut 12
20 × 20

Window patches
Cut 14
6 × 6

Denim
Cut 20
6 (1)

Side piece   Cut 4
30 / 2.5 / 13

Strip   Cut 2
8 (1.5) (1.5) — 32

Gusset / Top Lining } Cut 1 each
8 (2) (2) — 91

Handle   Cut 2
7 — 80

Pocket   Cut 1
15 (2) — 22

Back   Cut 2
30 Fold / 2.5 — 23

1

Make two

2

6.5cm (Include 1cm seam allowance)

Pin and baste triangle window patches at top and bottom and sew gusset between front and back.

Gusset

Gusset

3

Seam allowance 1cm

13cm

Pocket

6cm

1.2cm

Sew pocket to lining and sew lining to gusset.

4

Slip-stitch

1.2cm

Insert inner bag into outer bag and slip-stitch together along each side.

5

6cm

Slip-stitch curved edges to triangle at top. Incase raw edges of inner and outer bags with 8cm wide strips.

6

3.5cm

4cm   4cm   4cm

Sew here.

Pineapple Table Center and Mat

MATERIALS:
For Table Center: Sheeting: light yellow green, 92cm by 56cm; dark yellow green, 70cm by 60cm. Cotton prints: 50cm by 30cm each for (a) and (e); 50cm by 20cm for (b); 30cm square for (c); 30cm by 20cm for (d). Thin layer of batting, 60cm square. Cotton fabric for base, 56cm square. For

Mat: Sheeting: lavender, 92cm square; purple, 92cm by 45cm. Cotton prints: 92cm by 50cm each for (a), (c) and (e); 60cm by 30cm for (f); 60cm by 25cm for (g); 40cm by 30cm for (h). Thick layer of batting, 64cm by 96cm. Cotton fabric for base, 62cm by 92cm.

Patterns for table center

Cut out adding 0.8cm secm allowance.

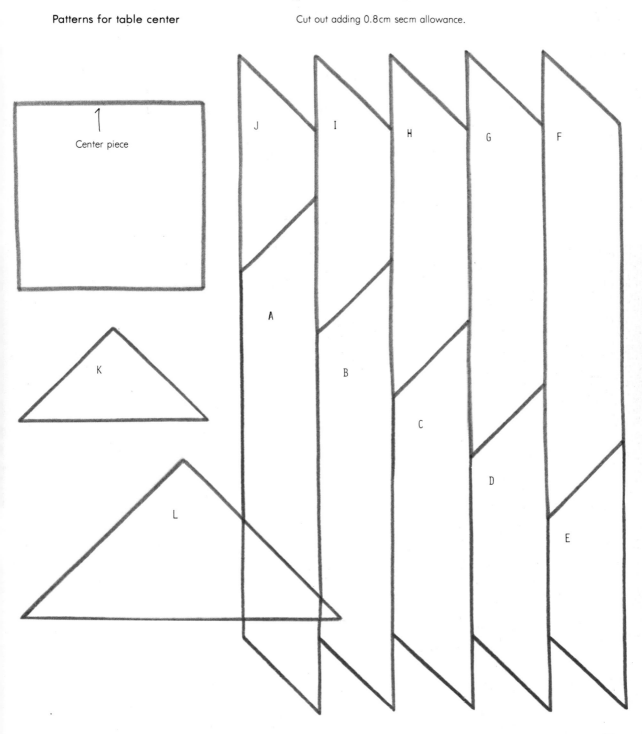

Patterns for mat

Cut out adding 0.8cm
seam allowance.

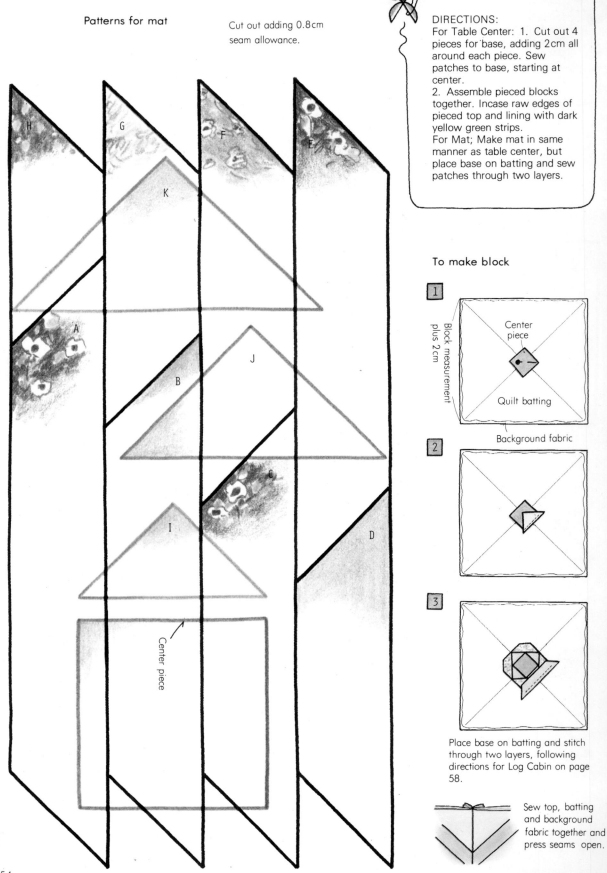

H

G

F

E

K

A

J

B

C

I

D

Center piece

DIRECTIONS:
For Table Center: 1. Cut out 4
pieces for base, adding 2cm all
around each piece. Sew
patches to base, starting at
center.
2. Assemble pieced blocks
together. Incase raw edges of
pieced top and lining with dark
yellow green strips.
For Mat; Make mat in same
manner as table center, but
place base on batting and sew
patches through two layers.

To make block

1

Block measurement
plus 2cm

Center
piece

Quilt batting

Background fabric

2

3

Place base on batting and stitch
through two layers, following
directions for Log Cabin on page
58.

Sew top, batting
and background
fabric together and
press seams open.

54

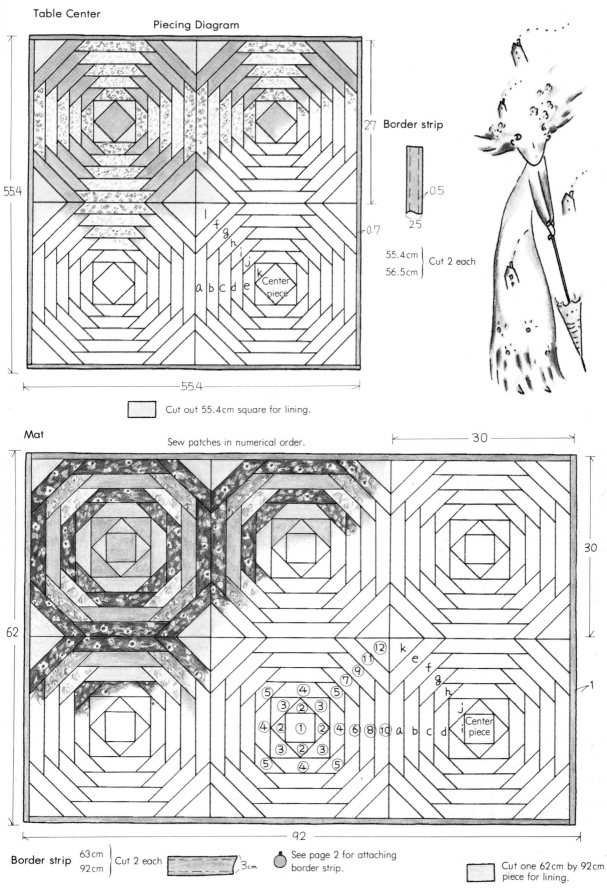

Table Center

Piecing Diagram

55.4

55.4

27 Border strip

0.5

2.5

0.7

55.4cm ⎫
56.5cm ⎭ Cut 2 each

l f g h i j k a b c d e Center piece

Cut out 55.4cm square for lining.

Mat

Sew patches in numerical order.

30

30

62

1

92

① ② ③ ④ ⑤ ⑥ ⑦ ⑧ ⑨ ⑩ ⑪ ⑫

k e f g h a b c d i j Center piece

Border strip

63cm ⎫
92cm ⎭ Cut 2 each

3cm

See page 2 for attaching border strip.

Cut one 62cm by 92cm piece for lining.

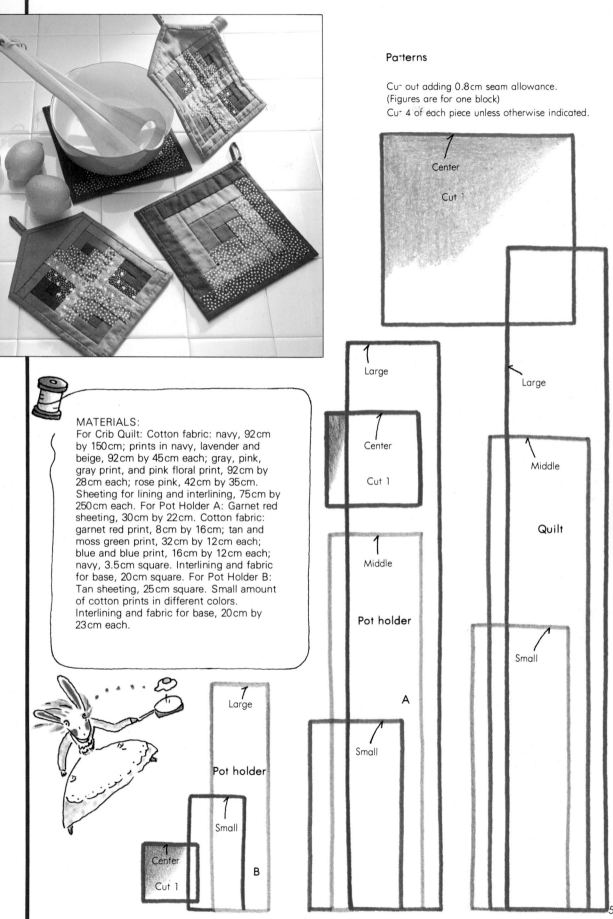

Patterns

Cut out adding 0.8 cm seam allowance.
(Figures are for one block)
Cut 4 of each piece unless otherwise indicated.

Center
Cut 1

Large

Center
Cut 1

Middle

Pot holder

A

Small

Large

Middle

Quilt

Small

Large

Pot holder

Small

Center
Cut 1

B

MATERIALS:
For Crib Quilt: Cotton fabric: navy, 92 cm by 150 cm; prints in navy, lavender and beige, 92 cm by 45 cm each; gray, pink, gray print, and pink floral print, 92 cm by 28 cm each; rose pink, 42 cm by 35 cm. Sheeting for lining and interlining, 75 cm by 250 cm each. For Pot Holder A: Garnet red sheeting, 30 cm by 22 cm. Cotton fabric: garnet red print, 8 cm by 16 cm; tan and moss green print, 32 cm by 12 cm each; blue and blue print, 16 cm by 12 cm each; navy, 3.5 cm square. Interlining and fabric for base, 20 cm square. For Pot Holder B: Tan sheeting, 25 cm square. Small amount of cotton prints in different colors. Interlining and fabric for base, 20 cm by 23 cm each.

To make Log Cabin Patch

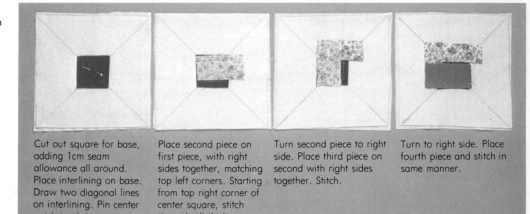

Cut out square for base, adding 1cm seam allowance all around. Place interlining on base. Draw two diagonal lines on interlining. Pin center patch in place.

Place second piece on first piece, with right sides together, matching top left corners. Starting from top right corner of center square, stitch through all thicknesses.

Turn second piece to right side. Place third piece on second with right sides together. Stitch.

Turn to right side. Place fourth piece and stitch in same manner.

DIRECTIONS for Crib Quilt:
1. Make blocks (a), (b), (c) and (d) as indicated, following directions for Log Cabin. Assemble blocks together.
2. Cut 5cm wide strip on the bias from navy and incase raw edges with strip.

Color key

Cut out adding 0.7cm seam allowance.

A
Make 9
— 20 —
20

B
Make 9

C
Make 6

D   Make 6

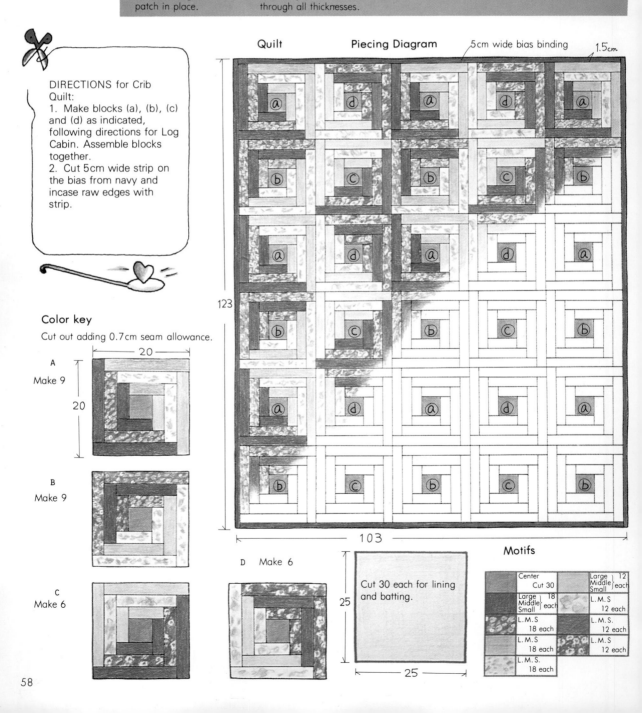

Quilt   Piecing Diagram   5cm wide bias binding   1.5cm

123

103

25

Cut 30 each for lining and batting.

— 25 —

Motifs

Center Cut 30		Large Middle Small	12 each
Large Middle Small	18 each	L.M.S	12 each
L.M.S	18 each	L.M.S.	12 each
L.M.S.	18 each	L.M.S.	12 each
L.M.S.	18 each		

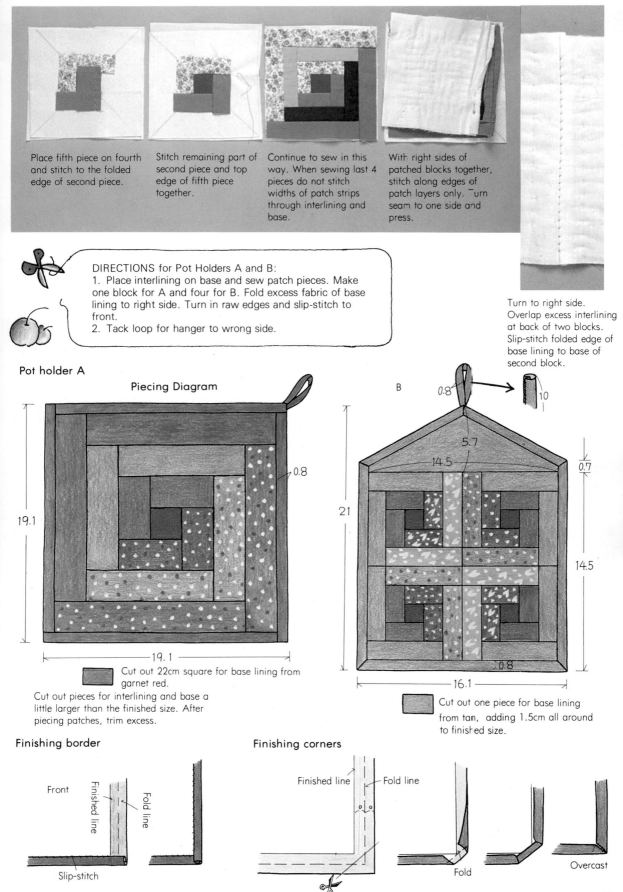

Place fifth piece on fourth and stitch to the folded edge of second piece.

Stitch remaining part of second piece and top edge of fifth piece together.

Continue to sew in this way. When sewing last 4 pieces do not stitch widths of patch strips through interlining and base.

With right sides of patched blocks together, stitch along edges of patch layers only. Turn seam to one side and press.

Turn to right side. Overlap excess interlining at back of two blocks. Slip-stitch folded edge of base lining to base of second block.

DIRECTIONS for Pot Holders A and B:
1. Place interlining on base and sew patch pieces. Make one block for A and four for B. Fold excess fabric of base lining to right side. Turn in raw edges and slip-stitch to front.
2. Tack loop for hanger to wrong side.

Pot holder A

Piecing Diagram

0.8

19.1

19.1

Cut out 22cm square for base lining from garnet red.

Cut out pieces for interlining and base a little larger than the finished size. After piecing patches, trim excess.

B

0.8

10

5.7

14.5

0.7

21

14.5

0.8

16.1

Cut out one piece for base lining from tan, adding 1.5cm all around to finished size.

Finishing border

Front

Finished line

Fold line

Slip-stitch

Finishing corners

Finished line

Fold line

Fold

Overcast

Kaleidoscope
Table Center
and
Place Mats

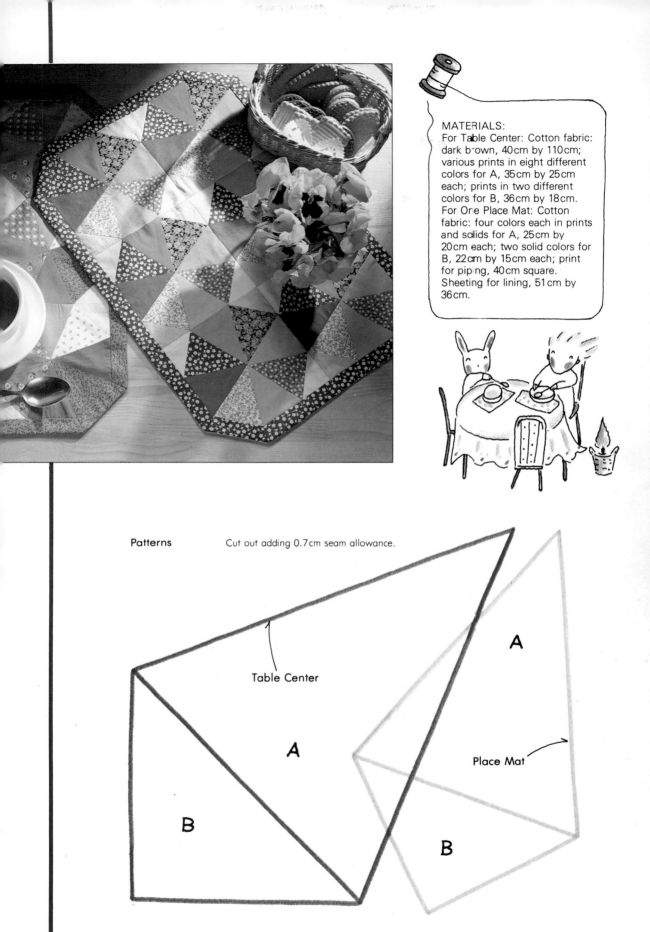

MATERIALS:
For Table Center: Cotton fabric: dark brown, 40cm by 110cm; various prints in eight different colors for A, 35cm by 25cm each; prints in two different colors for B, 36cm by 18cm.
For One Place Mat: Cotton fabric: four colors each in prints and solids for A, 25cm by 20cm each; two solid colors for B, 22cm by 15cm each; print for piping, 40cm square.
Sheeting for lining, 51cm by 36cm.

Patterns   Cut out adding 0.7cm seam allowance.

Table Center

A

A

B

B

Place Mat

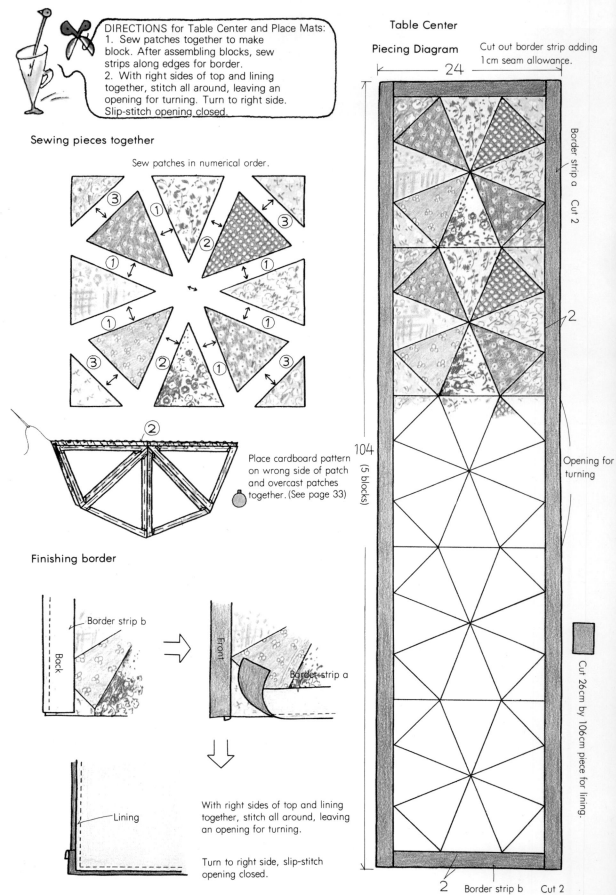

DIRECTIONS for Table Center and Place Mats:
1. Sew patches together to make block. After assembling blocks, sew strips along edges for border.
2. With right sides of top and lining together, stitch all around, leaving an opening for turning. Turn to right side. Slip-stitch opening closed.

Sewing pieces together

Sew patches in numerical order.

③ ① ③
②
① ①
① ①
③ ② ③
①

②

Place cardboard pattern on wrong side of patch and overcast patches together. (See page 33)

Finishing border

Border strip b

Back

Front

Border strip a

With right sides of top and lining together, stitch all around, leaving an opening for turning.

Lining

Turn to right side, slip-stitch opening closed.

Table Center

Piecing Diagram

Cut out border strip adding 1cm seam allowance.

24

Border strip a   Cut 2

2

104 (5 blocks)

Opening for turning

Cut 26cm by 106cm piece for lining.

2   Border strip b   Cut 2

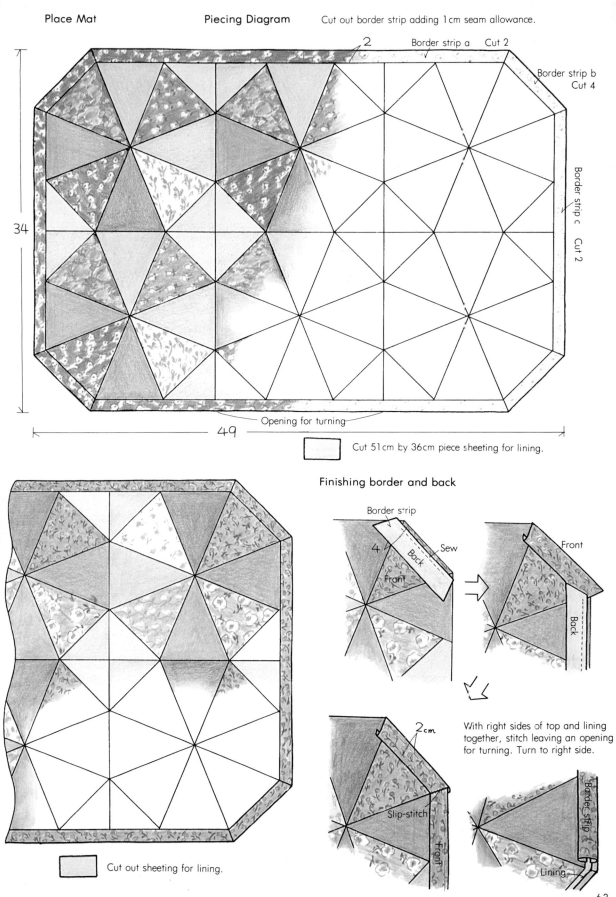

Place Mat   **Piecing Diagram**   Cut out border strip adding 1cm seam allowance.

2   Border strip a   Cut 2

Border strip b
Cut 4

34

Border strip c   Cut 2

49

Opening for turning

Cut 51cm by 36cm piece sheeting for lining.

Cut out sheeting for lining.

Finishing border and back

Border strip

4   Sew

Back

Front

Front

Back

2cm

Slip-stitch

Front

Border strip

Lining

With right sides of top and lining together, stitch leaving an opening for turning. Turn to right side.

Saw Tooth Crib Quilt, Framed Patchwork and Mat

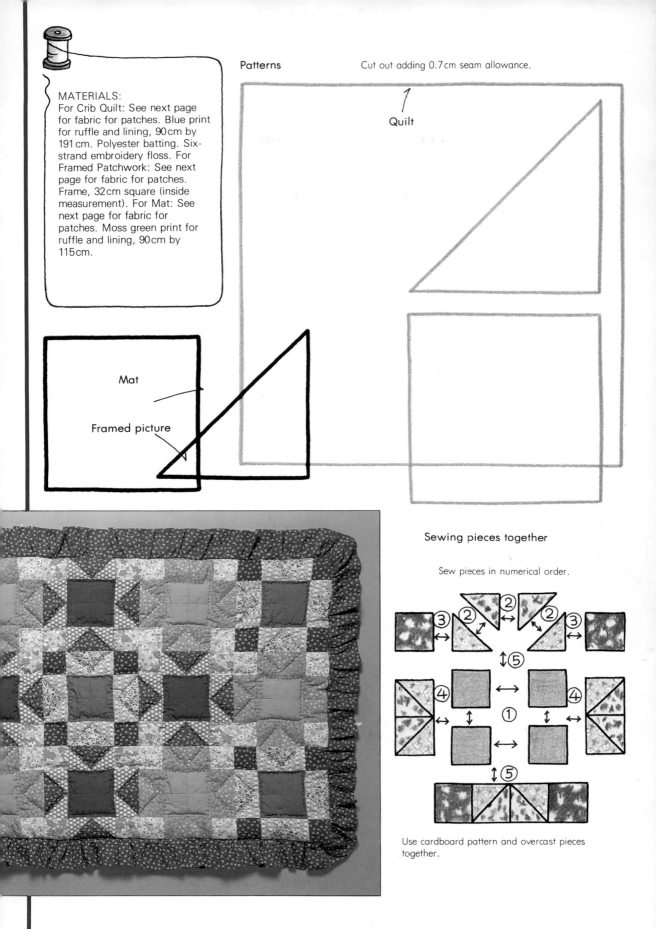

MATERIALS:

For Crib Quilt: See next page for fabric for patches. Blue print for ruffle and lining, 90cm by 191cm. Polyester batting. Six-strand embroidery floss. For Framed Patchwork: See next page for fabric for patches. Frame, 32cm square (inside measurement). For Mat: See next page for fabric for patches. Moss green print for ruffle and lining, 90cm by 115cm.

Patterns   Cut out adding 0.7cm seam allowance.

Quilt

Mat

Framed picture

Sewing pieces together

Sew pieces in numerical order.

Use cardboard pattern and overcast pieces together.

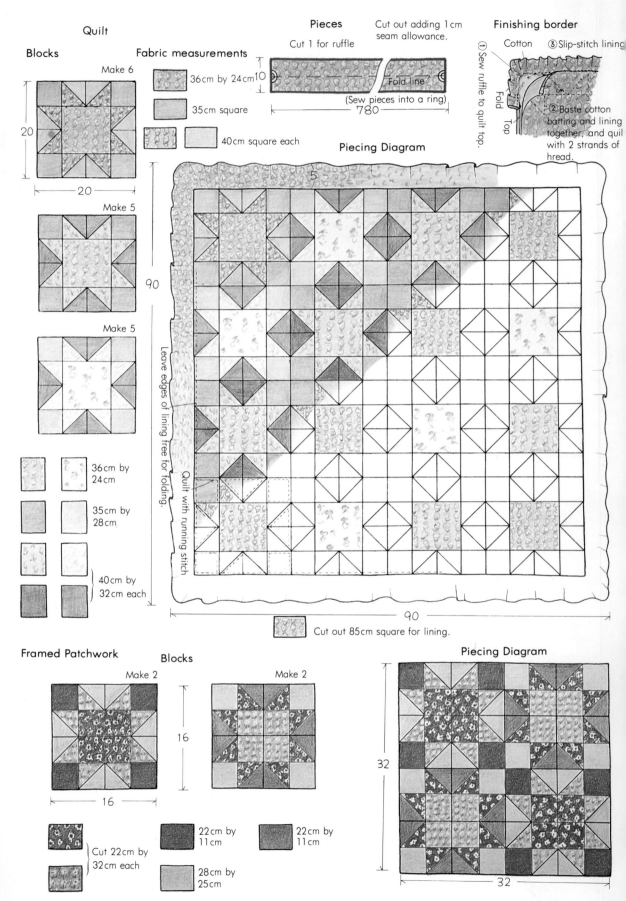

Quilt

Blocks

Make 6

20 × 20

Make 5

Make 5

Fabric measurements

36cm by 24cm
35cm square
40cm square each

36cm by 24cm
35cm by 28cm
40cm by 32cm each

Pieces

Cut 1 for ruffle

Cut out adding 1cm seam allowance.

Fold line

(Sew pieces into a ring)

780

10

Finishing border

Cotton

① Sew ruffle to quilt top.

③ Slip-stitch lining

Fold

Top

② Baste cotton batting and lining together, and quil with 2 strands of hread.

Piecing Diagram

5

90

90

Leave edges of lining free for folding.

Quilt with running stitch

Cut out 85cm square for lining.

Framed Patchwork

Blocks

Make 2

16 × 16

Make 2

Cut 22cm by 32cm each

22cm by 11cm

22cm by 11cm

28cm by 25cm

Piecing Diagram

32 × 32

66

DIRECTIONS:

For Crib Quilt: 1. After assembling quilt top, sew folded ruffle to quilt top all around.
2. Pin and baste quilt top, batting and lining together. Quilt along quilting lines, using two strands of embroidery floss. Leave edges of lining free for folding.

3. Turn in raw edges of lining and slip-stitch in place.
For Mat: Make mat in same manner as quilt.
For Framed Patchwork: Sew patches together and frame.

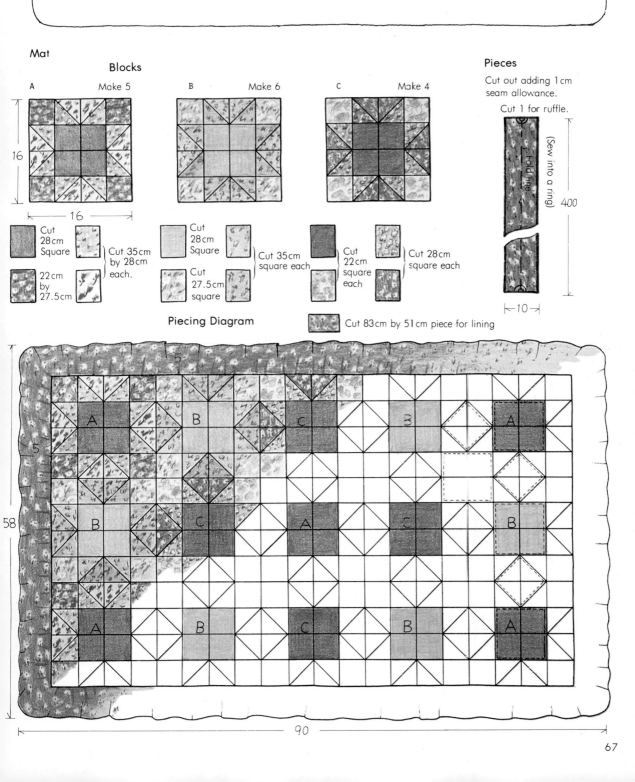

Mat

Blocks

A   Make 5   B   Make 6   C   Make 4

16

16

Pieces

Cut out adding 1 cm seam allowance.

Cut 1 for ruffle.

(Sew into a ring)

400

Fold line

10

Cut 28cm Square

22cm by 27.5cm

Cut 35cm by 28cm each.

Cut 28cm Square

Cut 27.5cm square

Cut 35cm square each

Cut 22cm square each

Cut 28cm square each

Piecing Diagram

Cut 83cm by 51cm piece for lining

5

5

58

90

**Tulip Wall Hanging,
Framed Patchwork
and Pochette**

MATERIALS:
For Wall Hanging: Sheeting: unbleached, 84cm by 126cm; golden yellow, 90cm by 284cm. Cotton fabric for patches: print for A, 48cm by 43cm; plain for B, 72cm by 30cm; print for C, 38cm by 30cm; prints for D and E, 50cm by 22cm each; plain for F, 21cm by 15.5cm. For Framed Patchwork: Cotton fabric: blue, 25cm by 30cm; 6.5cm by 10.5cm each for A and B; 11.5cm by 5.5cm each for C, D, E, F and G; 8.5cm by 2.5cm for H. Frame 20cm square (inside measurement). For Pochette: Cotton fabric: purple, 30cm by 20cm; pink, 14cm by 20cm; 9cm by 7cm each for A and B; 13cm by 4cm each for C, D, F and G; 7.5cm by 4.5cm for E; 6cm by 6.5cm for H; print for piping, 50cm square. Polyester batting. One large snap fastener. 4-ply yarn.

Sewing pieces together

Sew patches in numerical order.

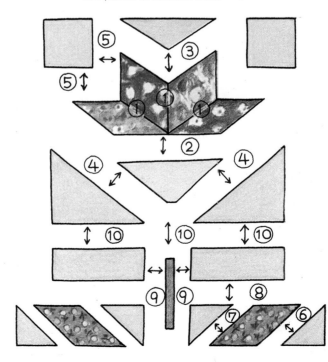

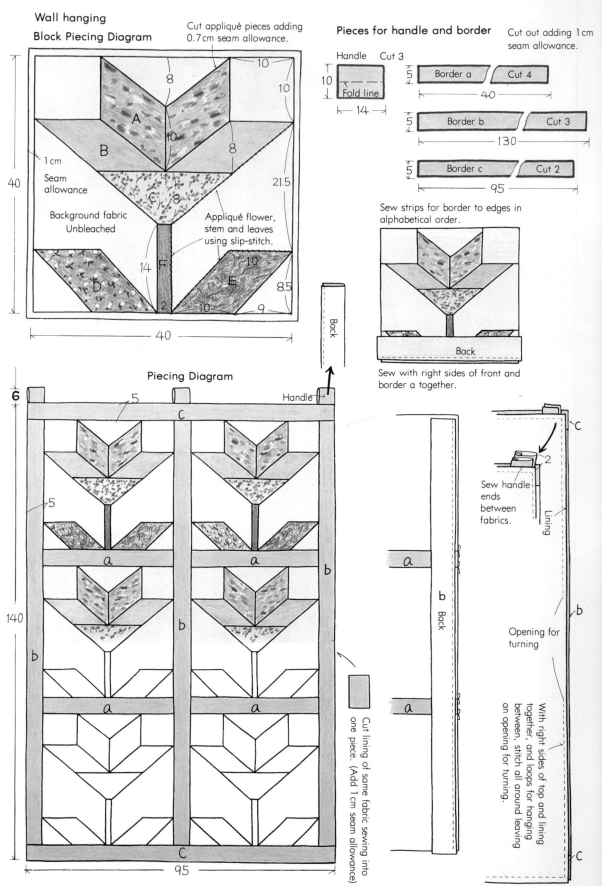

Wall hanging
Block Piecing Diagram

Cut appliqué pieces adding 0.7 cm seam allowance.

A

B
1 cm
Seam allowance

Background fabric
Unbleached

C   8

Appliqué flower, stem and leaves using slip-stitch.

D

F   14

E

8
10
10
10
8
10
21.5
10
8.5
9
2
40
40

Pieces for handle and border   Cut out adding 1 cm seam allowance.

Handle   Cut 3
10   14
Fold line

Border a   Cut 4   5   40
Border b   Cut 3   5   130
Border c   Cut 2   5   95

Sew strips for border to edges in alphabetical order.

Back

Sew with right sides of front and border a together.

Back

Piecing Diagram

6   5   Handle   C
5
b
a   a
b   b
a   a
C
140
95

Handle

Back
a
b   Back
a

C
Sew handle ends between fabrics.   2
Lining
b
Opening for turning
C

With right sides of top and lining together, and loops for hanging between, stitch all around leaving an opening for turning.

Cut lining of same fabric sewing into one piece. (Add 1 cm seam allowance)

70

DIRECTIONS:

For Wall Hanging: 1. Make patterns for patches as indicated. Appliqué pieced patches to background fabric.
2. Make six appliquéd squares. Assemble squares with short and long strips as shown. With right sides of top and lining together, stitch all around leaving an opening for turning.
For Framed Patchwork: 1. Sew patches together. Press seams open. Appliqué to background fabric. Frame.

For Pochette: 1. Sew patches together and appliqué to background fabric. Assemble other pieces together to make front. Insert thin layer of batting between front and lining.
2. Insert batting between back and lining. Incase raw top edges of front and back opening with strips.
3. With wrong sides of front and back together, incase remaining raw edges with one strip. Attach handle.

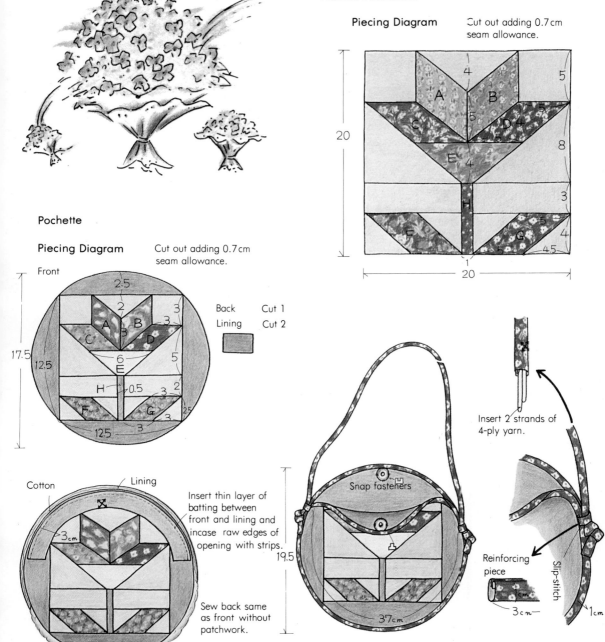

Framed Patchwork

Piecing Diagram — Cut out adding 0.7 cm seam allowance.

Pochette

Piecing Diagram — Cut out adding 0.7 cm seam allowance.

Front

Back — Cut 1
Lining — Cut 2

Insert 2 strands of 4-ply yarn.

Cotton — Lining

Insert thin layer of batting between front and lining and incase raw edges of opening with strips.

Sew back same as front without patchwork.

Snap fasteners

Reinforcing piece

Slip-stitch

71

Schoolhouse Pillows and Tote Bags

MATERIALS:

For Pillow: Use materials in parenthesis for blue pillow. Cotton prints: pink (blue), 84cm by 40cm; purple (blue), 32cm by 12cm; black (black), 21.5cm by 3cm. Plain cotton: dark pink (bluish gray), 21.5cm by 7.5cm; pink (blue), 24.5cm by 10cm; lavender (lavender), 23cm by 6.5cm; purple (purple), 9cm by 4.5cm. Cotton bias binding tape in cobalt blue, 165cm long. Inner pillow stuffed with 350g of kapok. 30cm zipper. Six-strand embroidery floss in pink (blue). For Bag A: Sheeting: pink, 90cm by 40cm; yellow green, 20cm by 12cm; beige, 12cm by 15cm. Cotton prints: green and pink, 40cm by 50cm each; light blue, 25cm by 22cm; blue, 8cm square. Six-strand embroidery floss in pink, yellow green, blue and beige. For B: Sheeting: gray, 62cm by 50cm; purple, 27cm by 10cm; grayish purple, 23cm by 10cm; dark pink, 10cm square; blue, 5.5cm by 5cm. Cotton prints: 90cm by 31cm for lining; white, 20cm square; blue, 43cm by 12cm. Six-strand embroidery floss in dark and light blue, pale blue, dark and light pink, golden yellow and green.

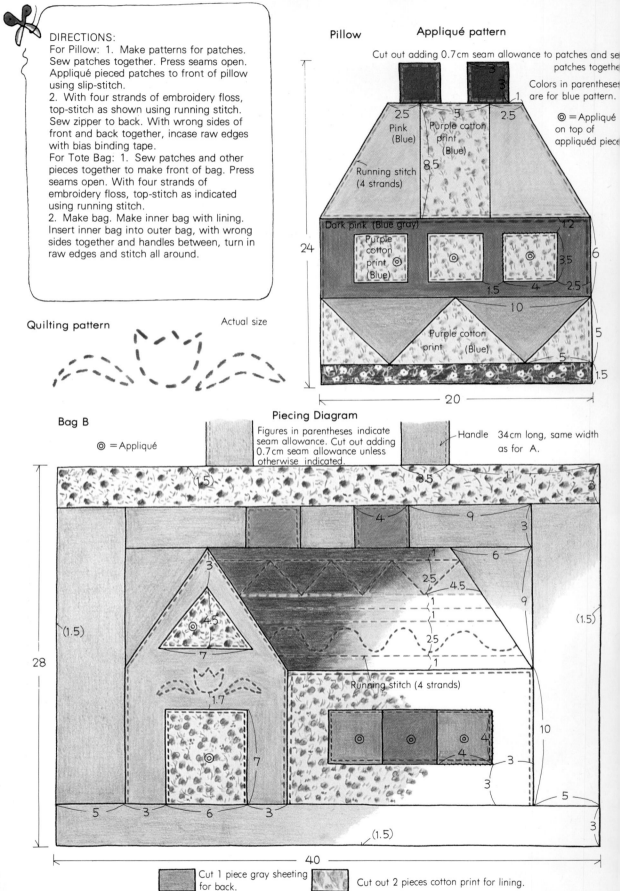

DIRECTIONS:
For Pillow: 1. Make patterns for patches. Sew patches together. Press seams open. Appliqué pieced patches to front of pillow using slip-stitch.
2. With four strands of embroidery floss, top-stitch as shown using running stitch. Sew zipper to back. With wrong sides of front and back together, incase raw edges with bias binding tape.
For Tote Bag: 1. Sew patches and other pieces together to make front of bag. Press seams open. With four strands of embroidery floss, top-stitch as indicated using running stitch.
2. Make bag. Make inner bag with lining. Insert inner bag into outer bag, with wrong sides together and handles between, turn in raw edges and stitch all around.

Quilting pattern

Actual size

Pillow

Appliqué pattern

Cut out adding 0.7cm seam allowance to patches and se patches together

Colors in parentheses are for blue pattern.

◎ = Appliqué on top of appliquéd piece

2.5 Pink (Blue)
5 Purple cotton print (Blue)
2.5
8.5
Running stitch (4 strands)

Dark pink (Blue gray)
Purple cotton print (Blue)
1.2
3.5
6
1.5
4
2.5

10
Purple cotton print (Blue)
5
5
1.5

24
20

Bag B

◎ = Appliqué

Piecing Diagram
Figures in parentheses indicate seam allowance. Cut out adding 0.7cm seam allowance unless otherwise indicated.

Handle 34cm long, same width as for A.

(1.5)
3.5
11
3
4
9
3
1
6
2.5
4.5
9
1
1
2.5
1
Running stitch (4 strands)
3
(1.5)
4.5
7
1.7
7
4
4
3
3
10
(1.5)
5
3
6
3
5
3
(1.5)

28
40

Cut 1 piece gray sheeting for back.
Cut out 2 pieces cotton print for lining.

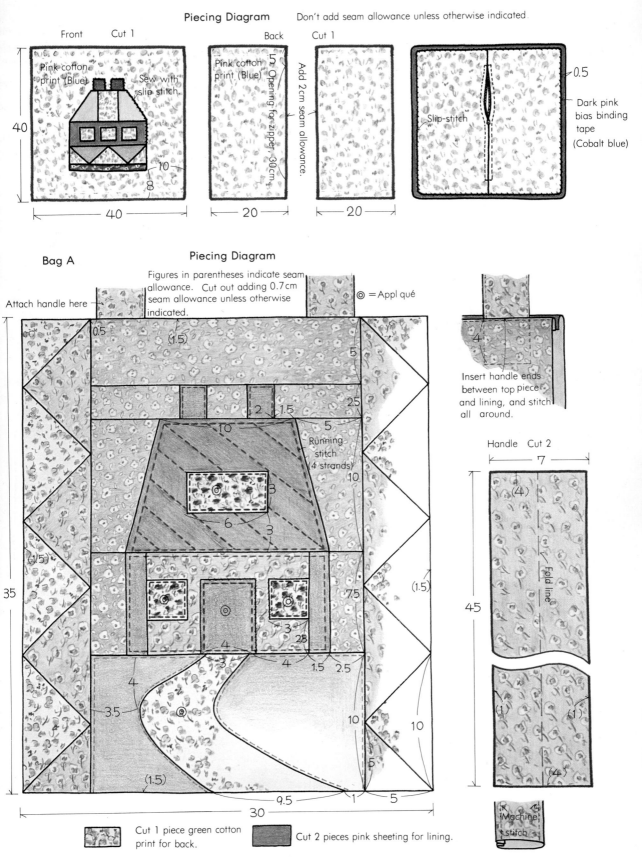

Piecing Diagram — Don't add seam allowance unless otherwise indicated.

Front — Cut 1
Pink cotton print (Blue)
Sew with slip stitch.
40
40
10
8

Back — Cut 1
Pink cotton print (Blue)
5
Opening for zipper, 30cm.
Add 2cm seam allowance.
20
20

Slip-stitch
0.5
Dark pink bias binding tape (Cobalt blue)

Bag A

Piecing Diagram

Figures in parentheses indicate seam allowance. Cut out adding 0.7cm seam allowance unless otherwise indicated.

◎ = Appliqué

Attach handle here

0.5
(1.5)
5
2.5
2
1.5
10
5
Running stitch (4 strands)
10
3
6
3
35
(1.5)
7.5
(1.5)
3
2.5
4
4
3
4
1.5
2.5
3.5
10
4
10
5
(1.5)
9.5
1
5
30

Insert handle ends between top piece and lining, and stitch all around.
4

Handle   Cut 2
7
(4)
Fold line
45
(1)
(1)
(4)

Machine stitch

Cut 1 piece green cotton print for back.

Cut 2 pieces pink sheeting for lining.

Flower Basket Tote Bags
and
Framed Patchwork Motifs

Patterns for bag and framed patchwork

Cut out adding 0.7 cm seam allowance.

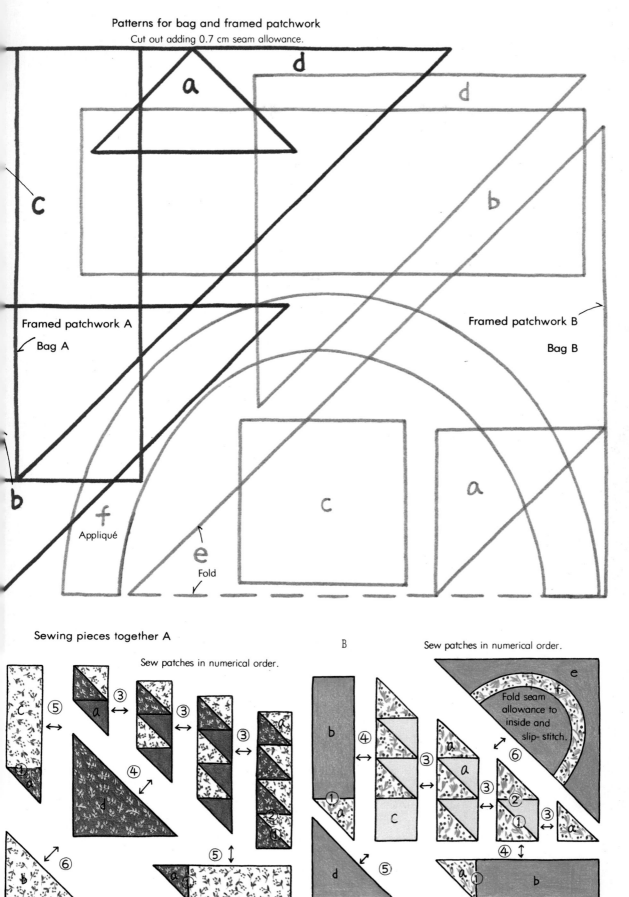

a

d

d

c

b

Framed patchwork A

Bag A

b

Framed patchwork B

Bag B

f

Appliqué

e

Fold

c

a

Sewing pieces together A

Sew patches in numerical order.

c ⑤

a ③ ③ ③

d ④

a ② ①

b ⑥

a ① ⑤

B

Sew patches in numerical order.

b ④

a ① c

a ③ a

③ a

Fold seam allowance to inside and slip-stitch. e f ⑥

② ① ③ a

d ⑤

a ① b ④

MATERIALS:

For Bag A: Heavyweight cotton fabric in navy, 92cm square. Cotton print for lining, 92cm by 65cm. Cotton fabrics for patches: navy print with white background and white print with navy background, 25cm by 20cm each; navy, 15cm square; red print with white background, 15cm by 10cm. For B: Unbleached canvas and beige cotton fabric for lining, 88cm by 65cm each. Cotton fabric: yellow green, 30cm square; for patches, yellow green and print with white background, 25cm square each, and beige, 13cm ssquare. For C: Unbleached quilted fabric, 60cm by 105cm. Cotton print for lining, 60cm by 85cm. Unbleached sheeting, 18cm by 19cm. Cotton fabrics for patches: yellow green, 30cm square; cream. 25cm square; green, 20cm square; red and gingham check, 15cm square each.

For framed patchwork motif A: Unbleached sheeting, 42cm by 22cm. Cotton print: navy blue, 22cm square; blue, 15cm square; yellow, 15cm by 10cm. For B: Unbleached sheeting, 50cm by 25cm. Cotton print: golden yellow, 25cm square. For C: Unbleached sheeting, 18cm square. Cotton fabrics: dotted print with white background, 20cm square; dotted print with red background, 15cm square; small dotted print with red backround, gingham check, print with white background, print with red background, 12cm by 6cm each. For all motifs: Polyester batting. White sewing thread.

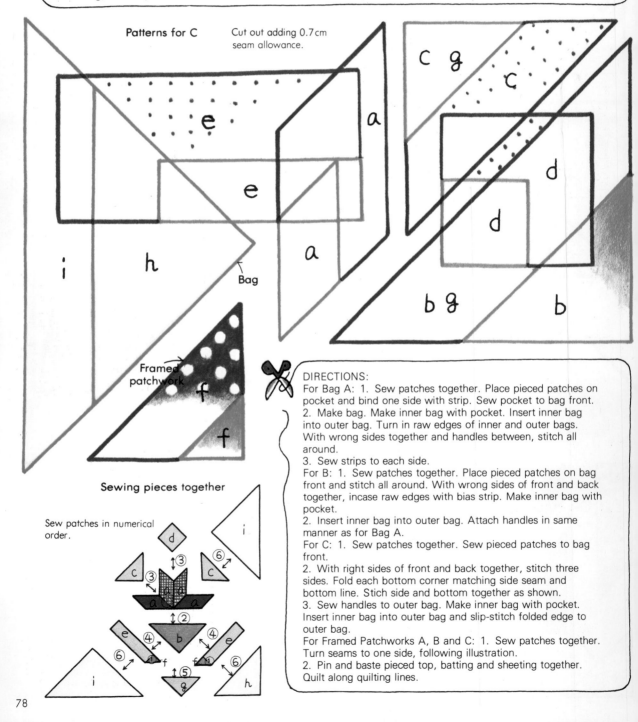

Patterns for C Cut out adding 0.7cm seam allowance.

Framed patchwork

Sewing pieces together

Sew patches in numerical order.

DIRECTIONS:

For Bag A: 1. Sew patches together. Place pieced patches on pocket and bind one side with strip. Sew pocket to bag front.
2. Make bag. Make inner bag with pocket. Insert inner bag into outer bag. Turn in raw edges of inner and outer bags. With wrong sides together and handles between, stitch all around.
3. Sew strips to each side.
For B: 1. Sew patches together. Place pieced patches on bag front and stitch all around. With wrong sides of front and back together, incase raw edges with bias strip. Make inner bag with pocket.
2. Insert inner bag into outer bag. Attach handles in same manner as for Bag A.
For C: 1. Sew patches together. Sew pieced patches to bag front.
2. With right sides of front and back together, stitch three sides. Fold each bottom corner matching side seam and bottom line. Stich side and bottom together as shown.
3. Sew handles to outer bag. Make inner bag with pocket. Insert inner bag into outer bag and slip-stitch folded edge to outer bag.
For Framed Patchworks A, B and C: 1. Sew patches together. Turn seams to one side, following illustration.
2. Pin and baste pieced top, batting and sheeting together. Quilt along quilting lines.

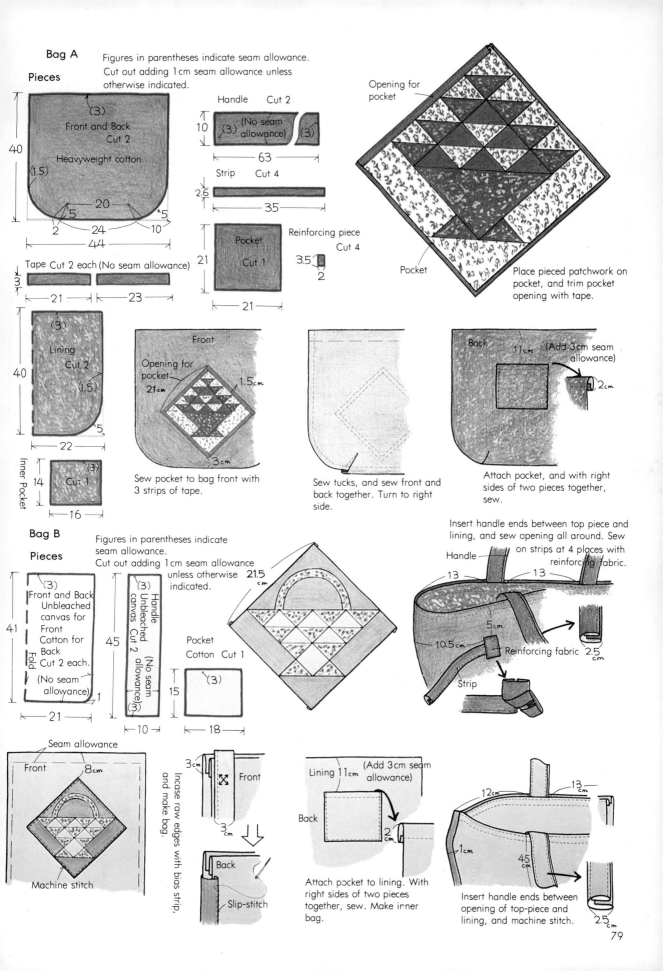

Bag A

Pieces

Figures in parentheses indicate seam allowance. Cut out adding 1cm seam allowance unless otherwise indicated.

(3)
Front and Back
Cut 2
Heavyweight cotton
40
(1.5)
20
5 5
2
24 10
44

Handle   Cut 2
10
(3) (No seam allowance)   (3)
63

Strip   Cut 4
2.6
35

Pocket
Cut 1
21
21

Reinforcing piece
Cut 4
3.5
2

Tape Cut 2 each (No seam allowance)
3
21
23

Opening for pocket

Pocket

Place pieced patchwork on pocket, and trim pocket opening with tape.

(3)
Lining
Cut 2
40
(1.5)
5
22

Inner Pocket
(3)
Cut 1
14
16

Front
Opening for pocket
21cm
1.5cm
3cm
Sew pocket to bag front with 3 strips of tape.

Sew tucks, and sew front and back together. Turn to right side.

Back
11cm
(Add 3cm seam allowance)
2cm
Attach pocket, and with right sides of two pieces together, sew.

Bag B

Pieces

Figures in parentheses indicate seam allowance. Cut out adding 1cm seam allowance unless otherwise indicated.

(3)
Front and Back
Unbleached canvas for Front
Cotton for Back
Cut 2 each.
(No seam allowance)
41
Fold
21
1

(3)
Handle
Unbleached canvas Cut 2
(No seam allowance)
(3)
45
10

Pocket
Cotton Cut 1
(3)
15
18

21.5 cm

Insert handle ends between top piece and lining, and sew opening all around. Sew on strips at 4 places with reinforcing fabric.

Handle
13   13
5cm
10.5cm   Reinforcing fabric 2.5 cm
Strip

Seam allowance
Front   8cm
Machine stitch

Incase raw edges with bias strip, and make bag.

3cm
Front
X
3cm

Back
Slip-stitch

(Add 3cm seam allowance)
Lining 11cm
Back
2cm
Attach pocket to lining. With right sides of two pieces together, sew. Make inner bag.

12cm   13 cm
45 cm
1cm
2.5 cm
Insert handle ends between opening of top-piece and lining, and machine stitch.

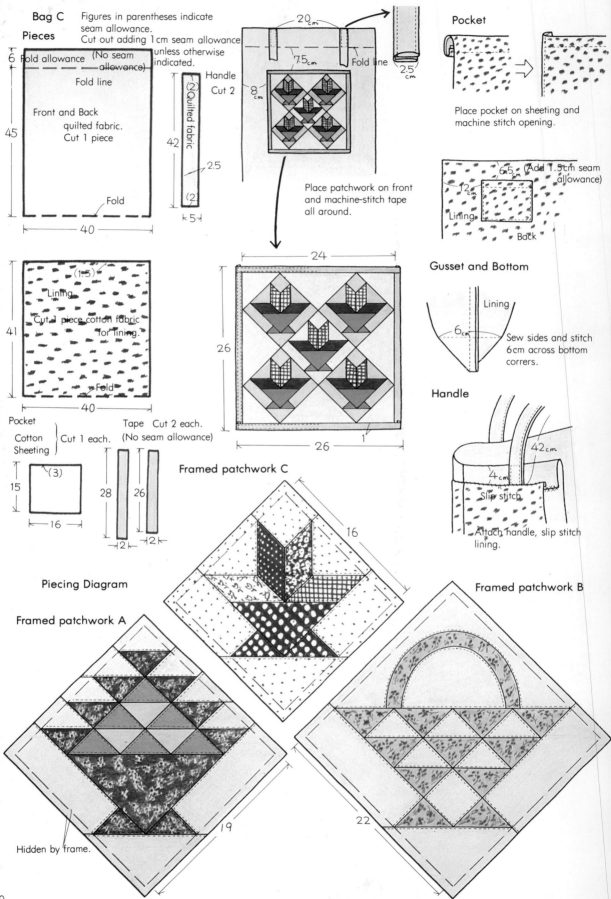

Bag C

Pieces

Figures in parentheses indicate seam allowance.
Cut out adding 1 cm seam allowance unless otherwise indicated. (No seam allowance)

6 Fold allowance
Fold line

Front and Back
quilted fabric.
Cut 1 piece

45

40

Fold

Handle
Cut 2

(2) Quilted fabric

42

2.5

(2)

5

20 cm

7.5 cm

8 cm

Fold line

2.5 cm

Place patchwork on front and machine-stitch tape all around.

Pocket

Place pocket on sheeting and machine stitch opening.

6.5 cm (Add 1.5cm seam allowance)

12

Lining

Back

Lining
(1.5)
Cut 1 piece cotton fabric for lining.

41

40

Fold

24

26

26

1

Framed patchwork C

Gusset and Bottom

Lining

6 cm

Sew sides and stitch 6cm across bottom corners.

Handle

42 cm

4 cm

Slip stitch

Attach handle, slip stitch lining.

Pocket
Cotton Sheeting } Cut 1 each.

Tape   Cut 2 each.
(No seam allowance)

15

(3)

16

28

26

2

2

Piecing Diagram

Framed patchwork A

Hidden by frame.

19

16

Framed patchwork B

22

80